THE ART OF POLITICS

A PRELUDE

N YANPOTHUNG EZUNG

Contents

CONTENTS

Acknowledgement

I would like to take this moment to extend my heartfelt appreciation to the remarkable people who have played crucial roles in bringing this book to live. Without their unwavering support, encouragement, and expertise, this endeavour would not have been possible.

First and foremost, I am deeply grateful to my family for their constant love, encouragement and understanding during the writing journey. Their unwavering belief in me has been a constant source of motivation throughout the challenging moments.

I would like to express my deepest gratitude to Shri. Mhathung Yanthan, Honorable MLA & Advisor for Agriculture, GoN for the sponsorship. I am also indebted to all my friends and colleagues who have generously offered their time, knowledge and encouragement. Your support has not only inspired me but has also added colour to this entire experience.

I extend my heartfelt thanks to Fr. Dr. Francis Cheerangal, Principal of St. Xavier College Jaluki, Peren, Shri. Imtitoshi, Commandant 12th NAP (IR) Chingtok, Longleng and T Mhathung Ezung, Vice Principal, GHSS, Mon Town for their mentorship, whose guidance and insightful feedback have been invaluable. Your wisdom and expertise have truly shaped this book into its current form, and I am immensely grateful for your patience and dedication throughout the process.

I would also like to thank Shri N Aremo Ngullie, Vice Principal, GHSS, Aghunato for his scrupulous efforts editing the whole manuscript without which the book would fall short of artistic flavour and interpretation. Your dedication, meticulousness and creativity have brought my work to life, and I am incredibly grateful to your hard work and commitment.

To those mentioned above and those inadvertently left unnamed, please accept my deepest appreciation for the roles you have played in bringing this book to fruition. Your contribution will forever hold a special place in my heart, and I am forever grateful for your support.

Thank you all sincerely.

Introduction

My apolitical nature has kept me away from active politics during my tender years of adulthood, having to miss out a lot of political opportunities. Later, I realised that hiding or running away from politics is a utopian dream. "Just because you do not take an interest in politics does not mean politics won't take an interest in you" by Pericles was an eye opener. "One of the penalties for refusing to participate in politics is that you end up being governed by your inferiors" by Plato triggered my attention to a large extend.

This book is the result of being in the political arena for considerable amount of years. Decade of observations and field experiences became the focal point of reference throughout the book but I intentionally kept myself away from writing a storytelling narrative.

Politics is a demanding and intricate field, yet it offers immense rewards. Whether aspiring to hold office, or work as a political consultant, or be a campaign manager, understanding the art of politics is crucial for playing along the power- corridor of politics.

This book aims to delve into the essential skills and strategies required to thrive in the realm of politics. It deals with various aspects, such as building a vital network, shaping one's public image, effectively communicating with constituents, and raising campaign funds. The focus will be on providing the fundamental knowledge needed to board on this journey.

Furthermore, this book explores the ethical and moral dilemmas that accompany a career in politics. Topics such as maintaining integrity and accountability, handling conflicts and disagreements, political leadership are some of the important features of this book. Plotting a route for the complex and entrancing world of politics requires careful consideration of these factors.

However this book has its limitations and shortcomings. It is based purely on my personal experience and notion, therefore any interpretations in this book which do not subscribe to the general understanding of the true nature of politics be set aside.

This book is intended to have a series of three- A Trilogy and hence sub titled as a Prelude. The book is therefore, fundamentally focused on the basics of political venture. The Intermezzo and the Finale is designed to go deeper into the more profound playfield of the game. Hopefully, let us wait what the future unfolds.

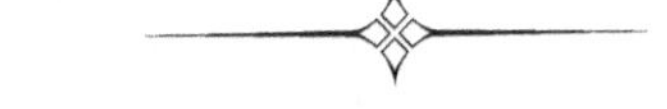

CHAPTER 1

Understanding Politics: The Basic Foundation

As someone deeply entrenched in the world of governance and policy-making, I've come to understand that politics, though a term frequently tossed around in casual conversation, is profoundly misunderstood by many. At its core, politics is the art and science of managing a country or organization's governance structure. This involves intricate decision-making processes that shape the allocation of power and resources, determine who gets to make these decisions, and outline the methods for resolving conflicts.

Politics weaves its threads, shaping the destinies of nations and individuals alike. Politics is not merely an abstract pursuit; it manifests itself in our everyday lives, impacting us in numerous ways. Political decisions have far-reaching consequences on our economies, communities, and personal freedoms. Therefore, it is vital to have thought-provoking insights and practical strategies to sail the often tumultuous waters of politics with confidence and purpose.

Politics is a dynamic and multifaceted realm that is pivotal in sculpting societal norms and governing structures. It involves a plethora of activities, actions, and policies that are aimed at acquiring and retaining power within governmental frameworks or influencing those in power. The essence of politics revolves around three core elements: the distribution of resources, the resolution of conflicts, and the exercise of authority.

Politics is not merely about the superficial play of power; it encompasses a deep study of various political institutions and ideologies that governs our society. Understanding the nuances of political behavior and power dynamics is essential for anyone looking to actively participate in shaping their community. By gaining insights into these elements, individuals are empowered to make informed decisions that contribute significantly to societal progress.

In politics, each decision and policy woven into the foundation of governance not only shapes the immediate scene but also casts long shadows over future generations. Thus, it is imperative for those involved in politics to operate with a blend of knowledge, wisdom, and ethical consideration, ensuring that their actions contribute positively to the collective future of their constituencies.

Influential Political theories

Being political or a politician need to muster up at least the basic concepts of politics and ideas behind those basic premises, on which they were build. Throughout history, a multitude of theories have arisen within political thought, molding our comprehension of governance, power dynamics, and societal structures. These theories stand as pillars upon which political frameworks and ideologies are constructed, guiding the paths of nations and civilizations. These theories represent the intellectual scaffolding upon which political structures and ideologies are built, shaping the course of nations and civilizations.

From the ancient wisdom of philosophers like Plato and Aristotle, who laid the groundwork for concepts such as democracy and republicanism, to the contemporary paradigms of liberalism, socialism, and conservatism, each theory offers distinct insights into the nature of authority, justice, and resource allocation within society.

Furthermore, these theories often emerge in response to pressing societal, economic, and cultural challenges, reflecting the evolving needs and aspirations of humanity across different eras. They provide lenses through which existing governance systems can be analyzed and critiqued, while also inspiring movements for reform and revolution.

Whether exploring the utilitarian principles of Jeremy Bentham, the revolutionary ideologies of Karl Marx, or the individualistic philosophies of John Locke, studying these political theories reveals the complex interplay between ideas and institutions in shaping human affairs.

By immersing oneself in these theories, one not only gains a deeper understanding of political dynamics but also acquires the critical tools needed to engage with contemporary issues and imagine alternative futures. Therefore, the exploration of these theories is indispensable for promoting informed citizenship, advancing social justice, and sailing the complexities of our interconnected world.

1. Classical Liberalism: Advocating Individual Freedom

Classical liberalism is a political philosophy and ideology that emerged in the 17th and 18th centuries, notably championed by thinkers such as John Locke, Adam Smith, and John Stuart Mill. At its core, classical liberalism advocates for primacy of individual freedom and limited government intervention in both economic and social affairs.

A cornerstone of classical liberal thought lies in the concept of natural rights that belong inherently to every individual. John Locke, for instance, argued that individuals possess certain unalienable rights—such as life, liberty, and property—simply by virtue of their humanity. These rights are not bestowed by the state but are rather intrinsic and pre-existing. Governments, according to classical liberals, are established to safeguard these rights and should refrain from unjustly infringing upon them.

Regarding economic policy, classical liberalism promotes the principles of free markets and limited government involvement in economic affairs. Adam Smith, often hailed as the pioneer of modern economics, advocated for free trade, private property rights, and the concept of the "invisible hand" guiding market forces. Smith believed that when individuals are allowed to pursue their self-interest through voluntary exchange, it leads not only to economic prosperity but also to overall societal advancement.

In matters of social governance, classical liberalism underscores the importance of individual autonomy and constraints on governmental authority. John Stuart Mill, in his seminal work "On Liberty," passionately defended the principle of individual sovereignty. He contended that individuals should enjoy the freedom to conduct their lives as they see fit, as long as their actions do not impinge upon the rights of others. This principle extends to matters of conscience, expression, and lifestyle choices, fostering a society marked by diversity, tolerance, and pluralism.

2. Marxism: Critiquing Capitalism and Class Struggle

Marxism is a socio-economic and political theory developed by Karl Marx and Friedrich Engels in the 19th century, which critique capitalism and emphasis the significance of class struggle in shaping society. At its core, Marxism posits that capitalism, an economic system where the means of production are privately owned and operated for profit, inherently leads to exploitation, inequality, and alienation.

Marxist critique of capitalism begins with the concept of private ownership of the means of production, such as factories, land and machinery. Marx argue that under capitalism, the bourgeoisie, or the capitalist class who own these means of production, exploit the proletariat, the working class, by extracting surplus value from their labour. This surplus value, in the form of profits, is appropriated by capitalists, leading to unequal distribution of wealth and resources.

Marx viewed capitalism as a system characterized by inherent contradictions and crises. Capitalism relies on constant expansion and accumulation of capital, which leads to overproduction, market instability, and economic downturns. These cyclical crises exacerbate social inequalities and deepens the exploitation of the working class.

Marxism also emphasizes the centrality of class struggle in driving historical change. Marx argued that throughout history, societies have been divided into antagonistic classes with conflicting interests. Under capitalism, the class struggle between the bourgeoisie and the proletariat is the primary motor of social transformation. Marx envisioned the eventual overthrow of capitalism by the working class, leading to the establishment of a classless society based on common ownership of the means of production, known as socialism or communism.

Marxism offers a comprehensive critique of capitalism, highlighting its inherent contradictions, exploitation of labour, and tendency towards crises. By emphasizing the importance of class struggle, Marxism provides a framework for understanding historical development and envisioning alternative socioeconomic systems based on equality, solidarity, and collective ownership.

3. Conservatism: Upholding Tradition and Stability

Conservatism, both a political and social ideology, is rooted in the preservation of traditional values, institutions, and social structures.

One key aspect of conservatism is its emphasis on tradition. Conservatives view traditions as repositories of wisdoms accumulated over generations, providing a sense of continuity and belonging to individuals and communities. They argue that traditions help foster social cohesion and stability by providing a framework within which individuals can understand their roles and obligations.

Stability stands as a cornerstone principle of conservatism. Advocates of conservatism prioritize order and predictability in societal affairs, contending that stability fosters economic prosperity and social harmony. They caution against abrupt or radical changes that may disrupt established norms, fearing potential chaos or unintended consequences.

Conservatism places a premium on individual responsibility and self-reliance, advocating for minimal government interference in both the economy and society. Free-market principles, limited government regulation, and fiscal prudence are championed as means to enhance individual freedom and prosperity, while upholding the traditional virtues of diligence and self-sufficiency.

Conservatism extends its advocacy to the defense of religious and cultural traditions, alongside skepticism towards rapid social change. Traditional family structures, gender roles, and moral values are viewed as vital components of societal stability, safeguarding against perceived cultural relativism or moral decline.

Conservatism revolves around the preservation of tradition and stability in society. It values the wisdom of the past, advocates for gradual change, prioritises the individual responsibility, and defends traditional values and institutions as essential pillars of social order and prosperity.

4. Feminism: Advocating Gender Equality

Feminism stands as a dynamic social and political movement advocating for gender equality across all spectrums of society, with a primary focus on addressing historical and systemic injustice faced by women. There lies a commitment to challenging and dismantling patriarchal norms and structures that perpetuate gender-based discrimination and oppression.

Central to feminism is the belief in the inherent worth and dignity of all individuals, regardless of gender. Feminists advocate for equal opportunities, rights, and representation in all spheres of life, including politics, economics, education, and the workplace. This includes addressing issues such as pay inequality, gender-based violence, reproductive rights, and access to healthcare.

Feminism acknowledges that gender inequality intersects with other forms of oppression, such as race, class, sexuality, and disability. Thus, feminists advocate for an inclusive and intersectional approach to activism, recognizing and amplifying the voices of marginalized individuals.

Feminist activism takes many forms, ranging from grassroots organizing and advocacy to legal reforms and cultural critique. Feminists work to raise awareness about gender inequality, challenge stereotypes and gender roles, and promote positive representation of women and marginalized genders in the media and popular culture.

Feminism extends its advocacy to encompass the rights of transgender and non-binary individuals, challenging binary understandings of gender and advocating for a society where individuals can express their gender identity authentically without fear of discrimination or violence.

In essence, feminism is a movement dedicated to achieving gender equality and justice for all individual, recognizing that true equality requires dismantling systemic barriers and challenging deeply ingrained societal norms and attitudes. Through collective actions and solidarity, feminists strive to create a more inclusive, equitable, and just world for everyone.

5. Socialism: Striving for Economic Equality

Throughout history, influential socialist thinkers like Robert Owen, Vladimir Lenin, and Rosa Luxemburg have scrutinized capitalist systems, proposing alternative economic models centered on cooperation, collective ownership, and equitable distribution of resources.

Socialism is driven by a commitment to addressing the perceived inequalities and injustices inherent in capitalism. By redistributing wealth and power more evenly among the populace, socialism seeks to create a fairer and more egalitarian society.

Socialism challenges the concentration of wealth and power in the hands of a privileged few under capitalism. It advocates for democratic control over economic decision-making processes to ensure that resources are utilized for the benefit of all members of society.

A fundamental tenet of socialism is the concept of collective ownership, which contrasts with the private control of industries and resources seen in capitalism. Socialism promotes various forms of ownership, including state ownership, worker cooperatives, and community-owned enterprises, aiming to eliminate exploitation and serve the common good.

Socialism prioritizes essential goods and services—such as healthcare, education, and housing—as universal rights rather than commodities driven by profit. By guaranteeing access to these necessities, socialism endeavors to combat poverty, reduce social disparities, and foster human well-being.

Socialism offers a vision for revitalizing society by advocating for collective ownership, economic equality, and social justice. By challenging entrenched capitalist systems and prioritizing the common good, socialism seeks to create a more equitable and flourishing world for all individual.

6. Liberal Democracy: Balancing Liberty and Equality

Liberal democracy represents a fusion of liberal principles and democratic governance, striving to harmonize individual freedoms with collective decision-making processes. Liberal democracy prioritizes the safeguarding of civil liberties, adherence to the rule of law, and the conduct of regular, free, and fair elections. Scholars such as John Stuart Mill and Alexis de Tocqueville have delved into the nuanced relationship between liberty and equality within liberal democratic frameworks, highlighting their convoluted interplay.

Liberal democracy endeavors to strike a delicate balance between the values of liberty and equality. It champions individual rights to freedom of speech, religion, assembly, and expression, while simultaneously recognizing the importance of ensuring equal opportunities and protections for all members of society.

Liberal democracy places a strong emphasis on the rule of law, which ensures that government actions are constrained by legal norms and principles. This helps to protect individual liberties from arbitrary encroachment by the state and promotes stability, predictability, and respect for basic human rights.

Liberal democracy features representative government, where political leaders are elected by the people to represent their interests and preferences. This allows for popular participation in decision-making and accountability of elected officials to the electorate. Additionally, liberal democracy often incorporate mechanisms for direct participation, such as referendums and initiatives, to further engage citizens in the political process.

While prioritizing individual liberty, it also endeavor to promote equality through various policies aimed at reducing socioeconomic disparities, ensuring access to essential services like education and healthcare, and combating discrimination on grounds of race, gender, religion, or other characteristics. Despite potential tensions between liberty and equality, liberal democracy takes the helm to these complexities through democratic deliberation, compromise, and respect for minority rights.

Liberal democracy stands as a dynamic framework that seeks to reconcile the values of liberty and equality within society. By upholding fundamental principles of civil liberties, rule of law, and representative governance, while actively promoting equality and social justice, liberal democracy strives to create inclusive, resilient, and flourishing societies.

7. Anarchism: Challenging Hierarchies and State Power

Anarchism emerges as a potent political ideology and philosophy that vehemently opposes centralized authority and hierarchical structures, advocating instead for a society founded upon voluntary cooperation and mutual aid.

Anarchist thinkers such as Pierre-Joseph Proudhon, Mikhail Bakunin, and Emma Goldman have scrutinized the oppressive mechanisms of the state and championed the abolition of unjust power structures. Anarchism encompasses a spectrum of ideologies, from individualist anarchism to anarcho-syndicalism, each offering unique perspectives on decentralized governance and liberation.

Anarchism fundamentally questions the legitimacy of centralized power structures, contending that they breed domination, exploitation, and the erosion of individual autonomy. This critique extends beyond governmental institutions to encompass all forms of hierarchy, including capitalism, patriarchy, and institutionalized discrimination.

Anarchism advocates for the dissolution of the state, deeming it inherently coercive and oppressive. Instead, anarchists endorse self-governance through voluntary associations and direct democracy. This decentralized approach promotes initiatives such as worker cooperatives, community councils, and grassroots social movements as viable alternatives to traditional hierarchical systems.

Anarchism encompasses a rich drapery of ideological currents, including mutualism, syndicalism, anarcha-feminism, and eco-anarchism. Despite varying analyses and strategies, these currents share a common goal: dismantling hierarchies of power and nurturing a society founded on principles of autonomy, cooperation, and voluntary association.

Critics often dismiss anarchism as impractical or utopian, arguing that it neglects the necessity of social institutions. However, proponents assert that anarchism offers tangible alternatives to systems of oppression and exploitation, rooted in values of freedom, equality, and solidarity.

8. Realism: Analyzing Power and International Relations

Realism stands as a pivotal theoretical framework within the realm of international relations, spotlighting the paramount importance of power dynamics in shaping the conduct of states and other global actors. Realist scholars like Hans Morgenthau and Kenneth Waltz assert that states are primarily driven by self-interest and the relentless pursuit of power. Their insights into the motivations behind state behavior offer valuable perspectives on the intricacies of global politics.

Realism underscores the significance of military strength, national security, and the equilibrium of power in influencing international relations. By prioritizing these elements, realism provides a lens through which to comprehend the complexities of conflicts and alliances among nations. Central to realism is the notion of an anarchic international system, wherein no overarching authority exists to enforce regulations or maintain order. In such an environment, states must rely on their own capabilities—particularly military and economic prowess—to safeguard their security and advance their interests.

Realism advocates for the principle of self-help, positing that states cannot afford to depend on external sources for their security. Instead, they must prioritize self-preservation and prosperity, often at the expense of rival states. This dynamic fosters behaviors such as military buildups, strategic alliances, and competitive maneuvering as states vie to bolster their relative power and influence.

Realism acknowledges the role of human nature in shaping international relations, contending that states are inherently self-interested and predisposed to conflict. This perspective underscores the competitive and sometimes zero-sum nature of global politics, where cooperation and diplomacy are often viewed through the prism of power and calculated self-interest.

9. Post-colonialism: Decolonizing Discourse and Identity

Post-colonialism stands as a critical lens through which to examine the enduring effects of colonialism and imperialism. Scholars like Edward Said, Frantz Fanon, and Gayatri Spivak have championed this framework, delving into the power dynamics between colonizers and the colonized.

Post-colonialism critiques Euro-centrism and confronts dominant narratives, aiming to dissect the complexities of identity, culture, and representation in today's world. It calls for a re-evaluation of historical records, advocating for social justice and equality.

Central to post-colonial thought is the recognition that colonialism isn't just a bygone era but an ongoing process that molds global inequalities and power dynamics. The exploitation and subjugation of colonized people have left behind entrenched hierarchies and stereotypes that persist to this day.

One of the primary goals of post-colonialism is to decolonize discourse and knowledge production. By challenging Eurocentric perspectives and amplifying marginalized voices, this framework aims to dismantle colonial biases ingrained in history, literature, and culture.

Post-colonialism seeks to deconstruct colonial identities and foster more inclusive forms of self-definition. This includes reclaiming suppressed indigenous languages, traditions, and cultural practices, while also challenging the imposition of Western norms as universal standards.

Post-colonialism invites us to confront the legacy of colonialism and work towards a more equitable future. By critically examining historical narratives and amplifying marginalized voices, we can begin to unravel the system of oppression that continues to shape our world.

10. Environmentalism: Advocating Ecological Responsibility

Environmentalism, a contemporary political ideology, underscores the pressing need for environmental conservation and sustainable behaviors. It confronts the ecological dilemmas arising from human actions and champions the protection of natural ecosystems and biodiversity. Visionaries in the environmental arena, such as Rachel Carson and Vandana Shiva, have spotlighted the detrimental consequences of industrialization and consumerism, urging collective efforts to combat climate change and promote ecological stewardship.

Environmentalism encompasses a diverse array of viewpoints, ranging from grassroots activism to policy advocacy and scientific inquiry. It tackles a myriad of environmental challenges, including climate change, pollution, deforestation, habitat loss, species extinction, and resource depletion.

Central to environmentalism is the principle of ecological responsibility, which acknowledges the finite nature of Earth's resources and accentuates the imperative of sustainable utilization. This necessitates adopting practices that minimize environmental harm, curb waste and pollution, and champion the conservation and regeneration of natural habitats.

Environmentalists advocate for policies and initiatives that promote renewable energy sources like solar, wind, and hydroelectric power, while advocating for reduced reliance on fossil fuels. Furthermore, they endorse endeavors aimed at safeguarding and rehabilitating ecosystems, such as reforestation endeavors, marine conservation projects, and land preservation endeavors.

A cornerstone of environmentalism is the dissemination of knowledge and awareness regarding environmental issues and their ramifications for human health, biodiversity, and the global climate. This entails fostering environmental literacy within educational institutions, conducting public outreach campaigns, and nurturing a culture of environmental mindfulness and accountability.

Environmentalism serves as a clarion call to safeguard our planet and ensure its well-being for generations to come. By embracing ecological responsibility, advocating for sustainable solutions, and promoting environmental awareness, we can collectively pave the way towards a more sustainable and harmonious coexistence with our natural world.

11. Nationalism: Emphasizing National Identity and Sovereignty

Nationalism emerges as a potent political ideology and sentiment, accentuating the significance of identity, culture, and sovereignty within a nation-state. It asserts the cohesive nature of a nation, bound together by shared communities such as language, ethnicity, culture, religion, or history. At its essence, nationalism cultivates a profound sense of belonging and allegiance among citizens towards their nation, often championing the ideals of national unity and cohesion.

Central to nationalism lies the emphasis on national identity, cultural legacy, and political autonomy. It advocates for prioritizing national interests over global or supranational affiliations. Influential nationalist scholars like Johann Gottfried Herder and Ernest Renan have delved into the role of language, culture, and collective history in shaping national consciousness. Notably, nationalism exhibits both positive and negative facets, shaping the formation of nation-states and influencing social dynamics.

Nationalism underscores the importance of promoting and preserving national identity, often reinforced through symbolic representations like flags, anthems, historical narratives, and cultural customs. Advocates of nationalism argue that nurturing a nation's identity is vital for fostering social cohesion and stability within its borders.

Sovereignty stands as a cornerstone of nationalism, signifying a nation's capacity to govern itself without external interference. Nationalists advocate for safeguarding their nation-state's autonomy and independence from external influences, including supranational bodies or foreign powers. This can manifest in policies aimed at defending borders, protecting national interests, and asserting authority over domestic affairs.

Nationalism manifests in various forms, spanning from civic nationalism, which emphasizes shared values and principles, to ethnic nationalism, which prioritizes ancestral ties and cultural heritage. While civic nationalism often promotes inclusivity and diversity, ethnic nationalism may lead to the exclusion or marginalization of minority groups based on ethnicity or cultural background.

Throughout history, nationalism has wielded significant influence, fueling movements for independence, self-determination, and nation-building. It has served as a unifying force, rallying people around common causes, yet has also incited conflicts and tensions between nations or within multi-ethnic societies.

Critics of nationalism contend that it can breed xenophobia, intolerance, and exclusivity, potentially promoting prejudice and discrimination against perceived outsiders. Moreover, in an increasingly interconnected world, excessive nationalism may impede international cooperation and dialogue, hindering efforts to address global challenges such as climate change, poverty, and conflict.

Nationalism evokes unity and pride among citizens, yet prompts reflection on inclusivity, diversity, and the delicate balance between national interests and international cooperation. As nations navigate the complexities of a globalized world, embracing nationalism alongside a commitment to global solidarity remains a paramount challenge for policymakers and citizens alike.

12. Utilitarianism: Maximizing happiness and well-being

Utilitarianism, a consequentialist ethical theory championed by philosophers such as Jeremy Bentham and John Stuart Mill, asserts that actions should be evaluated based on their capacity to maximize overall happiness or well-being. This consequentialist approach contends that the moral merit of an action hinges upon its consequences, advocating for the pursuit of the greatest good for the greatest number. Utilitarianism has exerted significant influence on ethical frameworks, public policy, and discussions surrounding welfare, justice, and resource allocation.

It focuses on the principle of utility, which states that the right action is the one that produces the most favourable balance of pleasure over pain or happiness over suffering. This principle treats happiness and well-being as the fundamental values to be pursued in ethical decision-making.

Utilitarianism advocates for a universal and impartial consideration of the interests of all individuals affected by an action, regardless of their personal relationships or social status. This approach prioritises the collective welfare over individual preferences or rights, emphasizing the importance of maximizing overall happiness across society.

One of the primary strengths of utilitarianism lies in its practicality and calculability. By focusing on measurable outcomes and quantifiable metrics of happiness and suffering, utilitarianism provides a systematic framework for evaluating moral dilemmas and making rational decisions. This consequentialist perspective enables individuals and policymakers to assess the potential benefits and drawbacks of various courses of action, ultimately selecting the option with the greatest overall utility.

Despite its merits, utilitarianism faces several criticisms. One notable concern revolves around the difficulty of accurately predicting the long-term consequences of actions, particularly in intricate and uncertain circumstances. Moreover, critics argue that utilitarianism may prioritize the interests of the majority at the expense of minority rights or individual autonomy, potentially resulting in unjust outcomes or the violation of moral principles.

Utilitarianism stands as a prominent ethical theory that continues to inform discussions on morality, public policy, and social justice. Its emphasis on maximizing happiness and well-being reflects a dedication to enhancing human welfare and advancing the common good across diverse contexts. Despite its imperfections, utilitarianism remains a pivotal framework for guiding moral complexities and striving towards a more equitable and flourishing society.

Types of politics

Types of Politics can be broadly categorized into two main branches: Domestic and International politics. Domestic politics pertains to the political activities and processes occurring within a country, encompassing aspects such as elections, public policy-making, and the functioning of government institutions. On the flip side, international politics revolves around the interactions and relationships between countries, covering areas like diplomacy, trade, and warfare.

Within the realm of domestic politics, various political systems exist. Democracy, for instance, is a governance structure where power is vested in the hands of the people through elections. In contrast, authoritarianism entails a system where power is concentrated in a single individual or group with limited accountability to the populace.

Key actors and institutions

Key actors and institutions play different roles depending on the type of political system in place. In a democracy, the primary actors are the people, while in an authoritarian system; the ruling elite wield the most influence. Irrespective of the political system, several crucial institutions significantly impact political dynamics.

Government stands out as the paramount institution in any political system, responsible for enacting laws, implementing policies, and delivering services to its citizens. Other influential institutions include political parties, interest groups, and the media, all possessing the ability to shape political outcomes.

Major issues and challenges

One of the prevailing challenges is the ascent of populism, an ideology emphasizing the concerns of ordinary people over those of the elite. Additionally, corruption, inequality, and climate change stand out as significant issues. Corruption erodes the legitimacy of government institutions, breeding widespread disillusionment among citizens. Inequality serves as a catalyst for social and political unrest, with marginalized individuals becoming increasingly vocal in their calls for change.

Political theories viv-a-vis politicians

The significance of political theories cannot be overstated for politicians. These theories offer a valuable framework that aids in comprehending the trivia of governance and the operation of political systems. Espousing ideologies like liberalism, conservatism, socialism, or feminism provides politicians with diverse insights, helping shape their decision-making processes.

One primary benefit of delving into political theories is the ability to articulate personal values and beliefs, constructing a cohesive political ideology. Familiarity with theories such as utilitarianism, social contract theory, or distributive justice empowers politicians to establish a robust foundation for their policy positions, facilitating effective communication of ideas to the public.

Studying political theories elevates a politician's critical thinking and analytical skills. This proficiency allows them to assess policies critically, evaluate the consequences of political decisions, and comprehend the potential outcomes of different approaches. Armed with this knowledge, politicians can make well-informed decisions, managing the complicated political landscape more adeptly.

Political theories also offer a historical context, aiding politicians in understanding the evolution of political systems. Delving into influential thinkers and theories across various periods sheds light on the underlying forces that have shaped past political events. This historical understanding provides valuable lessons, guiding future decision-making for effective governance.

In political debates and discussions, being familiarized with political theories equips politicians with a common language and theoretical foundation. This enables them to engage in meaningful discourse and effectively respond to opposing views. Armed with well-reasoned arguments, politicians contribute to constructive dialogue, providing effective governance and policy development.

Beyond providing a foundation, political theories serve as a wellspring of inspiration, offering alternative visions of society. The likes of Marxism, feminism, or environmentalism present fresh perspectives on social issues, leading to innovative policy proposals and approaches. For politicians, this inspiration translates into the ability to advocate for change and drive initiatives that enhance society.

In essence, politics transcends mere electoral victories; it embodies the commitment to serve constituents and advocate for meaningful change. Political theories furnish politicians with the requisite knowledge and tools to pilot the complexities of leadership and policymaking, ultimately facilitating the delivery of desired results.

Political participation

Political participation encompasses a wide array of activities through which individuals engage with the political process, influence decision-making, and express their preferences within a society. These activities can take various forms, ranging from voting in elections to participating in protests, volunteering for political campaigns, joining interest groups, contacting elected representatives, and even running for office. Political participation is a fundamental aspect of democratic governance, as it provides avenues for citizens to voice their concerns, shape public policies, and hold their leaders accountable.

At the heart of political participation lies the act of voting. Voting in election is one of the most common and direct ways for individuals to participate in the political processes. It allows citizens to choose representatives who will make decisions on their behalf, ranging from local council members to national leaders. However, voter turnout rates vary significantly across different states and regions, influenced by factors such as political culture, socioeconomic status, accessibility of polling stations, and the perceived effectiveness of elections in bringing about change.

Beyond voting, political participation includes activities that occur both within and outside formal political institutions. For example, joining political parties allows an individual to influence party platforms and candidate selection processes. Parties serve as vehicle for collective action, mobilizing supporters around shared ideologies and policy goals. Moreover, participating in party primaries and conventions enables members to shape the direction of the party and nominate candidates for public office.

Another form of political participation is engaging in advocacy and lobbying efforts. Interest groups, representing diverse interests such as environmental conservation, labour rights, or business interests, play a crucial role in shaping public policy. They organise campaigns, lobby lawmakers, and mobilise public support to influence legislation and regulatory decisions. By joining or supporting these organisations, individuals can amplify their voices and advocate for issues they care about.

In addition to formal channels of political participation, citizens often engage in informal activities to express their political preferences and influence public discourse. This can include participating in public demonstrations, signing petitions, boycotting products or services, or engaging in online activism through social media platforms. These forms of protest and dissent serve as important mechanism for citizens to express dissatisfaction with government policies or societal injustices, and they can catalyze broader social and political movement for change.

Political participation encompasses activities aimed at holding elected officials accountable for their actions. This can involve monitoring government performances, attending town hall meetings, writing letters to elected representatives, or filling freedom/right of information request to access government records. By staying informed and actively engaging with elected officials, citizens can ensure that their voices are heard and their concerns are addressed in the policymaking process.

Political participation extends beyond the domestic sphere to include engagement with international institutions and global issues. Citizens can participate in transnational advocacy networks, international conferences, or diplomatic negotiations to address global challenges such as climate change, human rights violations, or armed conflicts. In an increasingly interconnected world, individuals have opportunities to influence decision-making at the international level and contribute shaping global governance structure.

It is important to recognise that not all forms of political participation carry equal weight or influence. Structural factors such as socioeconomic status, education level, race, gender, and geographic location can shape individuals' access to and effectiveness within the political system. Historically marginalized groups often face barriers to participation and may resort to alternative tactics, such as grassroots organizing or direct action, to challenge systemic inequalities and empower their communities.

Moreover, technological advancements have transformed the scenario of political participation, providing new tools and platforms for civil engagement. Social media platforms, online petition websites, and digital communication tools have enabled individuals to connect with like-minded activists, coordinate collective action, and disseminate information on a massive scale.

However, digital technologies also raise concerns about privacy, misinformation, and the concentration of power in the hands of tech companies, which can impact the dynamics of political participation in complex ways.

Political participation encompasses a broad spectrum of activities through which individuals engage with the political process, influence decision-making, and express their preferences within a society. From voting in elections to joining interest groups, participating in protests, and engaging in online activism, citizens have various avenues to contribute to the functioning of democratic governance. However, disparities in access and influence persist; highlighting the importance of addressing structural barriers and promoting inclusive forms of participation that empower all members of the society to shape their collective future.

Political processes

Political processes encompass the mechanisms and dynamics through which societies govern themselves, make decisions, and resolve conflicts. These processes are fundamental to the functioning of political systems, shaping the distribution of power, the formulation and implementation of policies, and the negotiation of interests within a society. Understanding political processes is essential for analyzing how government operates, how policies are developed and enacted, and how individuals and groups engage with the political system to pursue their interest and values.

At the core of political processes is the concept of governance, which refers to the exercise of authority and the management of public affairs by institutions and individuals within a society. Governance structures vary widely across different political systems, ranging from authoritarian regimes with centralized control to democratic systems characterized by checks and balances, separation of powers, and the rule of law. Regardless of the specific form of governance, political processes shape how power is distributed, how decisions are made, and how resources are allocated within a society.

One key aspect of political processes is the formulation and implementation of public policies. Policymaking involves identifying societal problems, setting goals, evaluating alternative course of action, and implementing measures to address those problems. This process typically involves multiple actors, including elected officials, government agencies, interest groups, and civil society organisations. Policymaking can occur through various channels, such as legislative processes, executive orders, administrative rulemaking, or judicial decisions, depending on the specific political context and institutional arrangements.

Legislative process play central role in policymaking within democratic systems, where elected representatives debate, amend, and enact laws that governs the society. This often involves a series of steps, including the introduction of bills, committee hearing, floor debates, and voting. The legislative process allows for the negotiation of competing interests and the formulation of policies that reflect the preferences of diverse stakeholders. However, legislative process can also be influenced by factors such as lobbying and public opinion, which can shape the outcome of policy debates and decisions.

Executive processes, on the other hand, involve the implementation and enforcement of laws and policies by government agencies and officials. The executive branch, led by the head of state or government, is responsible for administering public services, managing public finances, and executing laws passed by the legislatures. Executive processes encompass a wide range of activities, including budgeting, planning, regulation, and law enforcement, which are essential for the functioning of government and the delivery of public goods and services.

Moreover, political processes encompass mechanisms for resolving conflicts and making decisions within a society. This can involve negotiation, mediation, or adjudication through formal institutions such as courts, arbitration panels, or regulatory agencies. Conflict resolution processes aim to reconcile competing interests, resolve disputes, and uphold the rule of law, thereby maintaining social order and stability. However, political conflicts can also manifest through non-institutional means, such as protests, strikes, or civil disobedience, which challenges existing power structures and demand change through collective action.

Another critical aspect of political processes is the role of the electoral systems and political parties in mediating between citizens and government. Electoral processes provide mechanisms for citizens to choose their representatives and hold them accountable through periodic elections. Electoral systems vary in their design, including first-past-the-post, proportional representation, or mixed systems, each with different implications for political representation, party competition, and government stability. Political parties serve as vehicle for aggregating and articulating the preferences of voters, mobilizing support, and competing for political power. They play a central role in shaping public opinion, organizing electoral campaigns, and formulating policy platforms, thereby influencing the direction of government policies and priorities.

Furthermore, political processes encompass mechanisms for public participation and engagement in decision-making. This can include public consultations, town hall meetings, citizen assemblies, or participatory budgeting initiatives, which allows individuals and communities to contribute to the policy making process and hold government accountable. Public participation enhances transparency, legitimacy, and responsiveness in governance, empowering citizens to shape the decisions that affect their lives and communities. However, barriers to participation, such as lack of information, unequal access to resources, or political marginalization, can limit the effectiveness and inclusiveness of these processes, undermining democratic ideals of representation and participation.

It operates within broader social, economic, and cultural contexts, which shape the dynamics of power, interests, and values within the society. Socioeconomic factors such as income inequality, unemployment, or social exclusion can influence political outcomes and processes, shaping patterns of participation, political behaviour, and policy priorities. Cultural factors such as language, religion, or ethnicity also play a role in shaping political identities, alliances, and conflicts, influencing the functioning of political institutions and processes.

Political processes encompass the mechanisms and dynamics through which societies govern themselves, making decisions, and resolve conflicts. From policymaking and conflict resolution to electoral competition and public participation, political processes shape the distribution of power, the formulation of policies, and the negotiation of interests within a society. Understanding these processes is essential for analyzing the functioning of political systems, assessing the legitimacy of the government actions, and promoting democratic governance that reflects the interests and values of all members of society.

Building Network:
Significance of Connections

Networking is the process of making connections and building relationships. These connections can provide advice and contacts which can be helpful in making informed decisions while building political network. The convoluted political milieu of the time demands the cultivation of robust relationships in molding outcomes and exerting influence over decisions. Whether one aspires to assume the mantle of a politician, an advocate, or merely harbors an interest in the political arena, comprehending the profound importance of networking and its consequential impact on their political trajectory is imperative. The adeptness in promoting and sustaining connections emerges as a linchpin for success. Spanning from grassroots activism to occupying upper echelons of governmental authority, individuals endowed with formidable networks often command substantial sway and authority.

Political networks epitomize a labyrinthine matrix of affiliations and interactions among individuals and factions within the political domain. These networks encompass a spectrum ranging from ad-hoc alliances forged during electoral campaigns to institutionalized frameworks within governmental apparatuses. A thorough comprehension of the dynamics inherent in political networks is indispensable for exploring the minutiae inherent in contemporary politics.

Political networking epitomizes an avenue for access – access to resources, intelligence, and decision-makers. Those endowed with extensive networks frequently enjoy privileged entry to policymakers, thereby enabling them to steer agendas, sculpt policies, and propel their personal interests forward. Furthermore, connections facilitate synergistic collaboration and coalition formation, empowering individuals to harness collective potency for mutual advancement. Cultivating a robust political network necessitates methodical endeavor and strategic cultivation of relationships. This entails nurturing authentic bonds grounded in trust, mutual esteem, and shared objectives. Networking functions, social congregations, and online platforms serve as conduits for expanding one's network, while sustained communication and follow-up are imperative for nurturing relationships over time.

Within electoral politics, networking emerges as a pivotal instrument for galvanizing support and resources. Candidates lean on their networks to muster volunteers, secure endorsements, and amass campaign finances. Moreover, grassroots organizers harness social networks and communal ties to build momentum and propel voter turnout. While networking constitutes an indispensable facet of political triumph, it is not devoid of ethical quandaries. Transparency, probity, and answerability loom large in promoting public trust and legitimacy. Politicians and public functionaries must negotiate potential conflicts of interest and circumvent the perception of undue influence or nepotism.

The scrutiny of triumphal network builders offers elucidation into efficacious strategies and optimal practices. Whether it is forging bipartisan coalitions or harnessing digital platforms for grassroots mobilization, these instances underscore the varied approaches to political networking. Despite its manifold benefits, political networking presents its fair share of challenges and perils. Preserving integrity in a cutthroat and frequently antagonistic milieu can prove arduous, while the perception of clandestine dealings or cronyism may erode public faith in the political process.

As technology continues to reshape the political panorama, the trajectory of political networking is undergoing a metamorphosis. Nascent trends such as data analytics, social media outreach, and online fundraising platforms are redefining the manner in which politicians interface with constituents and rally support. However, these innovations beget fresh ethical considerations and regulatory hurdles that demand redressal.

Constituting networks in politics transcends the realm of mere acquaintanceship; it hinges upon how one leverages those connections to instigate change and propel one's objectives. By cognizing the significance of connections, embracing ethical precepts, and assimilating novel technologies, political actors can direct the complexities inherent in modern politics with integrity and efficacy.

Networking: Connecting beyond the self

Networking has evolved into an integral aspect of both our personal and professional lives, serving as a conduit for connecting, collaborating, and cultivating valuable relationships. At its essence, networking involves establishing and nurturing connections with individuals who share similar interests, goals, or professional backgrounds. This process entails building a network that provides support, guidance, and collaborative opportunities, unfolding in various settings such as social events, conferences, online platforms, and professional organizations.

A robust network has the potential to unlock plethora of opportunities.

Moreover, networking offers an array of advantages, impacting both personal and professional spheres. It serves as a gateway to expanding knowledge and gaining insights from diverse perspectives. Engaging in meaningful conversations, exchanging ideas, and learning from experts across various fields become possible through networking. Connecting with individuals from diverse backgrounds and experiences broadens the horizon thus, opening a more comprehensive understanding of the world.

Networking goes beyond mere socializing; it emerges as a strategic instrument capable of shaping political trajectories, influencing decision-making processes, and unveiling a multitude of avenues for advancement. Whether in the pursuit of political aspirations or seeking to grasp the minutiae of the political process, recognizing and actively engaging in networking is a key element for success.

The Power of Networking

The significance of networking is profound, serving as the conduit through which politicians and others gain entry to pivotal resources, information, and decision-making circles. It facilitates the exchange of ideas, alliances, and support structures, empowering stakeholders to wield influence and mold outcomes.

Primarily, networking grants access to valuable resources, ranging from financial backing to logistical support. Political candidates, for instance, rely on their networks to secure campaign funds, recruit volunteers, and access expertise in various fields. Similarly, established politicians leverage their connections to garner support for legislative endeavors, procure government contracts, or mobilize resources for community projects.

Moreover, networking furnishes insider information and profound insights into the workings of the politics. Through informal dialogues, meetings, and strategic partnerships, individuals gain access to intelligence concerning forthcoming policy decisions, prevailing public sentiment, or potential obstacles. This knowledge empowers them to anticipate and respond effectively to changing circumstances, thereby enhancing their strategic advantage.

Furthermore, political networking facilitates the cultivation of relationships with key decision-makers and influential figures. By making alliances with fellow politicians, community leaders, or interest groups, politicians can amplify their voice, secure endorsements, and rally support for their agendas. These connections also serve as invaluable assets in navigating bureaucratic complexities, negotiating compromises, and forging consensus on contentious issues.

The potency of networking lies in its capacity to furnish access to resources, information, and influential personalities. Through the strategic leveraging of connections, both individuals and collectives can propel their interests forward, shape policies, and exert considerable sway over the political terrain.

Expanding Spheres of Influence

The sphere of influence in political networking is expanding rapidly, driven by technological advancements, evolving communication channels, and shifting societal dynamics. Traditionally confined to closed-door meetings and face-to-face interactions, political networking now transcends geographical boundaries and infiltrates diverse spheres of influence.

A primary catalyst for this expansion is the proliferation of digital platforms and social media. Politicians and activists alike utilize online networking to engage constituents, disseminate information, and mobilize support. Platforms such as Twitter, Facebook, and Instagram afford unprecedented global reach, enabling individuals to connect with audiences worldwide. Additionally, digital networking promotes direct communication between political leaders and constituents, enhancing transparency and governance accountability.

The emergence of data analytics has transformed political networking strategies. Campaigns and advocacy groups employ sophisticated algorithms to target specific demographics, tailoring messages to resonate with diverse audiences. Through comprehensive data analysis, stakeholders refine outreach efforts, optimize resource allocation, and maximize impact.

The globalization of political issues has expanded networking opportunities. Geopolitical events, economic policies, and environmental challenges transcend national borders, necessitating collaboration among stakeholders worldwide. International summits, diplomatic forums, and transnational partnerships serve as networking platforms, facilitating collaboration to address shared concerns and pursue common goals.

The democratization of information empowers grassroots movements and marginalized communities to influence political networking. Social justice movements, environmental activists, and advocacy groups leverage grassroots organizing and online mobilization to amplify their voices and drive change. Through collective action, these grassroots networks challenge established power dynamics and advocate for progressive reforms.

The sphere of influence in political networking is expanding rapidly, propelled by technological innovation, global interconnectedness, and grassroots activism. As traditional barriers dissolve and new avenues for engagement emerge, stakeholders must adapt their networking strategies to monitor and take advantage of this evolving scenario effectively. By approving digital platforms, leveraging data-driven insights, and managing inclusive partnerships, individuals and groups can extend their reach and amplify their impact on the political stage.

Mobilizing Support for Success

Mobilizing support stands as a foundational pillar of triumph in political networking, facilitating the aggregation of resources, endorsements, and popular approval for personal and collective endeavors. The efficacy of mobilization tactics hinges upon the adept utilization of persuasive discourse, grassroots mobilization strategies, and calculated coalition-building endeavors aimed at invigorating backing and furthering political aims.

Political actors must articulate a coherent vision, espousing values, and delineating concrete action plans to tackle pertinent issues. By framing their message in relatable terms and emphasizing shared concerns, they can instill trust and enthusiasm among the supporters.

Grassroots mobilization assumes a critical role in cultivating support from the grassroots level. Politicians deploy a spectrum of grassroots methodologies including door-to-door canvassing, phone banking, and community engagement initiatives to cultivate a cadre of committed volunteers and activists. These grassroots networks serve as the backbone of political movements, facilitating the mobilization of resources, dissemination of awareness, and stimulation of voter participation.

Cultivating strategic alliances with influential stakeholders amplifies the impact of mobilization endeavors. Seeking endorsements from notable figures within their constituency, encompassing elected officials, community leaders, and advocacy groups, enhances the credibility of their endeavors and broadens appeal across diverse demographics.

The mobilization of support emerges as indispensable for success in political networking, necessitating a multifaceted approach amalgamating persuasive rhetoric, grassroots mobilization, and strategic collaborations. Through the crafting of compelling narratives, cultivation of grassroots networks, formation of strategic partnerships, and adept utilization of digital platforms, politicians endeavor to catalyze support, mobilize resources, and attain objectives within the intricate terrain of contemporary politics.

Strategic Connections for Electoral Impact

In the pursuit of electoral influence through political networking, strategic connections serve as a cornerstone. Within the electoral domain, politicians recognize the pivotal role of forging alliances and affiliations to mobilize support, garner endorsements, and secure victory at the polls. These connections are meticulously cultivated through strategic planning, relationship cultivation, and coalition-building endeavors aimed at maximizing electoral sway.

Harnessing strategic connections for electoral impact involves identifying key stakeholders who wield considerable influence over voter sentiments and outcomes. This includes elected officials, community leaders, interest groups, and influential individuals within targeted demographics. By meticulously mapping out the political terrain and pinpointing potential allies and supporters, politicians or candidates can adapt their outreach endeavors and prioritize engagement with those possessing the greatest potential to sway public opinion.

Once these key stakeholders are identified, politicians focus shift towards nurturing alliances and coalitions that align with their policy objectives and electoral aspirations. This entails proactive outreach to potential partners, establishing common ground, and negotiating mutually advantageous agreements. These strategic alliances may manifest in various forms, including formal endorsements, joint campaign activities, and collaborative fundraising initiatives. By uniting forces with like-minded entities, politicians aim to amplify their message, expand their appeal, and consolidate support across diverse constituencies.

Endorsements from esteemed figures and organizations hold considerable sway in electoral campaigns, signifying credibility, legitimacy, and public backing. Candidates actively seek endorsements from elected officials, community leaders, advocacy groups, and influential individuals who can sway voter perceptions and mobilize their respective constituencies. Endorsements serve as a stamp of approval, lending credibility to candidates' platform and enhancing their visibility and electability.

Candidates cultivate relationships with local activists, volunteers, and community organizers who can mobilize resources, spread awareness, and galvanize voter turnout. Grassroots networks harness the power of door-to-door canvassing, phone banking, and community outreach to engage with voters on a personal level, build rapport, and drive support for the candidate's campaign.

Political networking extends beyond traditional avenues to encompass online engagement and social media outreach. Candidates leverage digital platforms such as X (Twitter), Facebook, and Instagram to connect with voters, disseminate messaging, and mobilize support. Strategic use of social media enables candidates to reach a wider audience, engage with constituents in real-time, and generate buzz around their campaigns. Moreover, digital networking facilitates fundraising efforts, volunteer recruitment, and voter outreach on a scale previously unimaginable.

While strategic connections are integral to electoral success, candidates must be mindful of ethical considerations and strive to avoid any perception of undue influence or favoritism. Transparency, integrity, and accountability are paramount in maintaining public trust and credibility. Candidates must uphold ethical standards in their interactions with stakeholders, disclose potential conflicts of interest, and adhere to campaign finance regulations to ensure fairness and transparency in the electoral process.

Strategic connections are essential for achieving electoral impact through political networking. By identifying key stakeholders, building alliances and coalitions, garnering endorsements, mobilizing grassroots support, and leveraging digital platforms, candidates can amplify their message, broaden their appeal, and mobilize resources to secure victory on Election Day. However, success in political networking must be tempered by ethical considerations to uphold the integrity and legitimacy of the electoral process.

Knowledge Sharing and Policy Enhancement

Networking goes beyond mere support; it acts as a conduit for the dissemination of knowledge. In political networking, the fusion of knowledge sharing and policy enhancement constitutes pivotal elements, facilitating the exchange of ideas, expertise, and optimal methodologies among stakeholders to inform decision-making processes, sculpt policies, and instigate progressive transformations.

Political networking serves as a nexus for knowledge exchange, empowering stakeholders to impart insights, experiences, and specialized knowledge on pertinent issues and policy dilemmas. Through informal dialogues, symposiums, and collaborative endeavors, policymakers, subject matter experts, and advocates disseminate invaluable information and research discoveries to enrich comprehension and stimulate policy deliberations. This culture of knowledge sharing cultivates innovation, encourages cross-sectoral collaborations, and augments the caliber of policy conceptualization and execution.

Furthermore, political networking assumes a pivotal role in policy refinement, nurturing dialogues and collaboration among heterogeneous stakeholders to identify lacunae, inefficiencies and avenues for amelioration within prevailing policies and initiatives. By congregating stakeholders from governmental bodies, academic circles, civil society and the private sector, policymakers harness collective expertise and diverse perspectives to conceive innovative remedies, streamline procedures, and tackle emergent challenges. Endeavors in policy refinement may encompass policy briefings, task forces, and collaborative research endeavors aimed at formulating evidence-based recommendations and policy overhauls.

Effective political networking involves engaging a broad spectrum of stakeholders, including policymakers, experts, advocacy groups, and affected communities, in policy discussions and decision-making processes. By soliciting input and feedback from diverse perspectives, policymakers can ensure that policies are responsive to the needs and priorities of the population they serve. Stakeholder engagement promotes transparency, accountability and inclusivity in the policymaking process, building trust and legitimacy in government institutions and decision-makers.

Moreover, political networking empowers stakeholders to champion policy imperatives and galvanize support for legislative endeavors. Through strategic partnerships, coalitions, and grassroots mobilization campaigns, advocacy groups and interest organizations amplify their voices, shape public sentiments, and wield influence over policy outcomes. By capitalizing on their networks and assets, advocates elevate awareness, garner momentum and catalyze action on pressing concerns, ultimately influencing policy determinations and catalyzing affirmative transformations.

Enhancing Visibility and Credibility

Enhancing visibility and credibility in political networking involves strategically positioning oneself or an organization to increase public awareness, trust, and perceived competence within the political arena. This process is essential for building influence, attracting support, and achieving success in political endeavors.

Enhancing visibility entails increasing the public awareness of one's presence, activities, and contributions within the political sphere. This can be achieved through various means, including media appearances, public speaking engagements, and participation in high-profile events. By actively engaging with the media and leveraging social media platforms, individuals and organizations can amplify their message, reach a wider audience, and shape public perceptions. Additionally, visibility can be enhanced through networking events, community outreach initiatives, and participation in political campaigns, allowing stakeholders to connect with constituents, stakeholders and decision-makers on a personal level.

Credibility pertains to the perceived trustworthiness, expertise, and reliability of an individual or organization in the eyes of others. Building credibility in political networking involves demonstrating integrity, competence, and consistency in one's actions and communications. This may entail maintaining transparency in decision-making processes, adhering to ethical standards, and delivering on promises made to constituents and stakeholders. Furthermore, credibility can be bolstered through the endorsement of respected leaders, experts, and institutions within the political community. Endorsements serve as a stamp of approval, lending legitimacy and credibility to one's reputation and initiatives.

Strategic communication is a key to enhancing both visibility and credibility in political networking. This involves engineering a cohesive and compelling narrative that highlights one's values, accomplishments, and vision for the future. By articulating a clear message and communicating it effectively across various channels, individuals and organizations can shape public perceptions, build trust, and differentiate themselves from competitors. Moreover, strategic communication involves actively listening to constituents' concerns, soliciting feedbacks, and addressing criticisms in a constructive manner, demonstrating responsiveness and accountability.

Consistency and authenticity are paramount in establishing credibility in political networking. It is imperative to align words with actions and maintain a consistent demeanor and message over time. Inconsistencies or contradictions can erode trust and undermine credibility, whereas authenticity brings connection and resonance with audiences. By staying true to one's values, principles, and commitments, individuals and organizations can build a reputation for integrity and reliability, enhancing credibility in the eyes of constituents and stakeholders.

Diplomacy and Consensus Building

Diplomacy and consensus-building constitute the bedrock principles underpinning effective political networking, serving as indispensable instruments for nurturing cooperation, mitigating conflicts, and propelling shared objectives within the political sphere. Diplomacy encapsulates the complex art of orchestrating negotiations, nurturing dialogue, and stewarding relationships among individuals, factions or nations to realize mutual comprehension and collaboration. In the milieu of political networking, diplomacy is deployed to drive multifarious interests, bridge schisms, and forge connections among stakeholders harboring competing agendas. This endeavor may encompass engaging in diplomatic dialogues, mediating disputes, and seeking common ground through the art of compromise and negotiation. The overarching aim of diplomatic endeavors is to nurture trust, engender goodwill, and lay the groundwork for synergistic initiatives that accrue benefits to all vested parties.

Concurrently, consensus building denotes the iterative process of attaining accord or consensus among stakeholders harboring divergent viewpoints or interests. It entails inclusive dialogues, soliciting inputs from a spectrum of stakeholders, and converging on common ground regarding contentious matters through constructive engagement and negotiation. Within political networking, consensus building necessitates adept facilitation, attentive listening, and a proclivity for exploring innovative solutions that accommodate the exigencies and apprehensions of all involved parties. By prioritizing consensus, stakeholders can engender widespread backing for policy imperatives, fortify relationships, and augment the legitimacy and durability of decisions undertaken.

In political networking, diplomacy and consensus-building are sine qua non for forging alliances, resolving conflicts, and propelling collective interests. Diplomacy empowers stakeholders to drive labyrinthine power dynamics, instill trust, and cultivate fruitful relationships with counterparts spanning ideological fault lines. Conversely, consensus building brings collaboration, galvanizes momentum, and promotes cohesion around shared aspirations. By harnessing diplomatic acumen and consensus-building strategies, political actors can surmount impediments, forge strategic partnerships, and effect substantive headway on pivotal issues, thereby underpinning effective governance and democratic equilibrium.

Access to Resources and Opportunities

Cultivating relationships with donors, party officials, and interest groups, individuals can mobilize resources to fund political campaigns, organize events, and implement strategic initiatives. Moreover, access to resources enables stakeholders to overcome barriers, seize opportunities, and steer challenges more effectively, thereby enhancing their competitiveness and viability in the politics.

Political networking also opens doors to a myriad of opportunities for personal and professional advancement. This may include access to leadership positions, committee assignments, speaking engagements, and policymaking roles within government institutions. By forging connections with influential decision-makers, individuals can position themselves for career advancement, appointment to key positions, and opportunities to shape policy outcomes. Moreover, networking enables individuals to stay informed about upcoming opportunities, such as job openings, grant opportunities, or collaborative partnerships, allowing them to capitalize on emerging trends and developments within the political sphere.

Trust, Reputation, and Mentorship

Trust forms the foundation of effective political networking, serving as the bedrock upon which relationships are built and sustained. Trust entails confidence in the integrity, reliability, and sincerity of one's counterparts. Trust is cultivated through consistent and transparent communication, mutual respect, and a demonstrated commitment to shared values and objectives. Political actors must manifest trustworthiness in their actions and interactions, honoring their commitments, and acting in the best interests of their constituents and stakeholders. By nurturing trust, individuals and organizations can forge enduring relationships, mobilize support, and take the helm of complex political dynamics with poise and legitimacy.

Reputation emerges as a paramount currency, molding perceptions, swaying decisions, and dictating one's status within the political echelon. A positive reputation is built through a track record of integrity, competence, and effective leadership. Political actors must cultivate a reputation for honesty, transparency, and accountability in their dealings with constituents, colleagues, and the public. A robust reputation bolsters credibility, fosters trust, and opens doors to new opportunities for collaboration and advancement. Conversely, a damaged reputation can undermine credibility, erode trust, and impede one's ability to achieve political objectives. Therefore, maintaining a positive reputation is paramount in political networking, requiring individuals to uphold ethical standards, deliver on promises, and demonstrate integrity in all aspects of their work.

Mentorship provides guidance, support, and opportunities for personal and professional development. Mentorship relationships often form between seasoned veterans and aspiring leaders seeking to drive the complexities of politics and advance their careers. Mentors dispense invaluable insights, impart wisdom gleaned from experience, and furnish constructive feedback to aid mentees in their journey toward growth and success. Mentorship bonds engender a culture of learning, collaboration, and perpetual refinement within the political fraternity, empowering individuals to surmount challenges, seize opportunities, and actualize their utmost potential. Moreover, mentorship promotes diversity and inclusion by providing underrepresented cohorts with access to guidance, resources, and networks that may otherwise be inaccessible. By investing in mentorship, political actors can cultivate the next generation of leaders, strengthen the fabric of the political community, and foster a culture of trust, respect, and collaboration that benefits all stakeholders.

Contributing to Social Capital

Political networking furthers the development of social connections and networks of support within communities. By engaging with constituents, grassroots organizations, and community leaders, political actors build relationships based on trust, reciprocity, and shared interests. These social connections form the foundation of social capital, facilitating collaboration, collective action, and the exchange of resources and information among community members.

Political networking enables individuals and groups to mobilize resources, rally support, and advocate for collective interests within society. Through strategic alliances, coalition-building efforts, and grassroots organizing, stakeholders pull their networks to address social, economic, and political challenges facing their communities. By working together, individuals can amplify their voices, influence decision-making processes, and effect positive change that benefits the broader community.

It builds trust and social cohesion within communities by promoting transparency, accountability, and inclusive decision-making processes. When individuals engage in political networking, they demonstrate a commitment to working collaboratively towards common goals, which promotes a sense of trust and solidarity among community members. This trust forms the basis for cooperation, reciprocity, and collective action, strengthening social bonds and enhancing resilience in the face of adversity.

Politicians, by identifying key stakeholders, leveraging various platforms, and actively engaging with diverse groups, create a robust network that enhances their influence, credibility, and ability to achieve their goals. Networking is a dynamic and ongoing process that requires dedication, active engagement, and a genuine commitment to building meaningful relationships within the political bubble. It stands as a powerful tool, enabling politicians to steer the complexities of politics, enhance effectiveness, increase chances of success, and make a lasting impact on the political landscape.

Is political networking different from other networking?

Political Networking: The primary purpose of political networking is to advance political objectives, such as gaining influence, building coalitions, and advocating for policy changes. Political networking focuses on connecting with stakeholders within the political sphere, including elected officials, government agencies, advocacy groups, and community organizations, to achieve specific political outcomes.

Commercial Networking: Commercial networking revolves around building business relationships and pursuing economic opportunities. The goal of commercial networking is to expand professional connections, generate leads, and promote business interests. It involves engaging with clients, suppliers, investors, and industry peers to facilitate transactions, collaborations, and growth in the business sector.

Social Networking: Social networking platforms are designed for connecting with friends, family, and acquaintances and sharing personal updates, photos, and interests. Social networking focuses on building personal relationships, staying connected with others, and cultivating a sense of community online. While social networking may involve political or commercial discussions, its primary purpose is social interaction and relationship building.

Audience and Engagement

Political Networking: Political networking targets individuals and organizations involved in politics, governance, and public policy. It often involves engaging with stakeholders who have decision-making authority or influence over political processes. Political networking requires a deep understanding of political dynamics, issues, stakeholders, and involves strategic communication and relationship-building efforts to advance political goals.

Commercial Networking: Commercial networking focuses on engaging with business professionals, entrepreneurs, and industry experts. It involves attending networking events, conferences, and trade shows, as well as participating in online forums and professional associations. Commercial networking emphasizes promoting products, services, and professional expertise to generate business opportunities and expand professional connections.

Social Networking: Social networking platforms cater to a broad audience of individuals from diverse backgrounds and interests. Users engage in social networking to connect with friends, share personal experiences, and participate in online communities.

Social networking platforms offer features for sharing content, interacting with others, and joining groups based on common interests, hobbies, or affiliations.

Communication and Interaction

Political Networking: Political networking often involves formal communication channels, such as meetings, conferences, and policy briefings, as well as informal interactions, such as receptions, dinners, and social gatherings. It may also include advocacy campaigns, lobbying efforts, and grassroots organizing to mobilize support and influence political decisions.

Commercial Networking: Commercial networking relies on various communication channels, including in-person meetings, phone calls, emails, and social media platforms. It encompasses activities such as networking events, business luncheons, and informational interviews to establish connections, exchange business cards, and explore potential collaborations or partnerships.

Social Networking: Social networking platforms facilitate communication through features such as posts, comments, likes, and direct messages. Users interact with others by sharing content, engaging in discussions, and participating in online communities. Social networking enhances informal communication and relationship-building through casual interactions and shared interests.

Legal and Ethical Considerations

Political Networking: Political networking often operates within the framework of legal and regulatory constraints governing political activities, such as campaign finance laws, lobbying regulations, and disclosure requirements. Ethical considerations are paramount in political networking, as stakeholders must adhere to ethical standards, transparency, and accountability to maintain public trust and legitimacy.

Commercial Networking: Commercial networking also operates within legal and ethical boundaries, such as anti-trust laws, privacy regulations, and industry-specific codes of conduct. Business professionals must comply with laws and regulations governing competition, consumer protection, and intellectual property rights while engaging in commercial networking activities.

Social Networking: Social networking platforms are subject to legal regulations governing data privacy, online harassment, and content moderation. Users must adhere to terms of service, community guidelines, and copyright laws when sharing content and interacting with others on social media. Ensuring the privacy and security of personal information is a critical ethical consideration in social networking.

Measurement and Evaluation

Political Networking: Political networking efforts are often evaluated based on tangible outcomes, such as policy changes, legislative victories, or electoral success. Metrics may include the number of bills passed, public opinion polls, or election results to assess the effectiveness of political networking strategies.

Commercial Networking: Commercial networking success is typically measured by business metrics, such as revenue growth, customer acquisition, or return on investment (ROI). Business professionals may track networking activities, such as leads generated, contracts secured, or partnerships formed, to evaluate the impact of commercial networking efforts.

Social Networking: Social networking success can be measured by engagement metrics, such as likes, shares, comments, and follower growth on social media platforms. Users may also assess the quality of social connections and interactions based on the depth of relationships, frequency of engagement, and relevance of content shared.

Integration and Synergy

Political Networking: Political networking may intersect with commercial and social networking efforts, particularly in areas where political, economic, and social interests converge. Integration of networking strategies can create synergies and amplify impact across different spheres, such as corporate social responsibility initiatives, public-private partnerships, or grassroots advocacy campaigns.

Commercial Networking: Commercial networking may overlap with political and social networking activities, as business professionals engage with policymakers, community leaders, and social influencers to advance business interests, support social causes, or shape public opinion.

Social Networking: Social networking bridges personal, professional and political spheres, as users steer diverse social connections and engage in discussions on a wide range of topics, including politics, business, and personal interests. Social networking platforms serve as hubs for connecting individuals and building communities around shared values, interests, and affiliations.

Networking—it is not just about awkwardly handing out business cards at stuffy events or schmoozing over rubbery chicken at conferences. No, networking is the secret sauce of success in both professional and personal realms. It is about building genuine connections, bringing collaboration, and creating opportunities for growth.

What is the Buzz about Networking?

Networking is a term that elicits both excitement and dread in equal measure. But Networking isn't as intimidating as it seems. At its core, networking is simply about building relationships and leveraging those connections to achieve common goals. Whether you're a seasoned professional or a newbie in the workforce, networking opens doors to new opportunities, insights, and perspectives.

Networking: Not Just for Extroverts

Contrary to popular belief, we don't need to be a smooth-talking extrovert to excel at networking. In fact, introverts possess unique strengths—such as active listening, deep reflection, and thoughtful communication—that can make them formidable networkers. So, whether we are the life of the party or the quiet observer in the corner, there's a place for us in the world of networking.

The Dos and Don'ts of Networking

Now that we've demystified networking, let's us try to figure out the dos and don'ts. But first, a word of caution: Avoid these networking faux pas at all costs unless you want to become the talk of the town (for all the wrong reasons).

Networking Dos

Be authentic: Don't try to be someone you're not. Authenticity is key to building genuine connections.

Listen more, talk less: Remember the 80/20 rule: Listen for 80% of the conversation and talk for 20%. People love to be heard.

Follow up: After making a new connection, don't forget to follow up with a personalized message or email. It shows that you value the relationship.

Give before you get: Instead of immediately asking for favors, offer help or resources to your network. Generosity goes a long way.

Networking Don'ts

Don't be overly aggressive: Nobody likes a pushy networker. Take a chill pill and let the conversation flow naturally.

Avoid monopolizing conversations: Remember, networking is a two-way street. Don't hog the spotlight; give others a chance to shine.

Don't forget to follow through: If you promise to connect someone with a contact or resource, make sure you follow through. Your reliability is on the line.

Avoid being inauthentic: Phony compliments and exaggerated stories will only backfire in the long run. Stay true to yourself.

Nurturing political networking

To maintain a prominent position in the political hierarchy, nurturing and continuous maintenance of networks are essential. Consider the following strategies for effective networking:

1. *Attend political events*: Actively participate in political conferences, rallies, fundraisers, and community gatherings. Engage with fellow politicians, activists, and constituents, initiating conversations to build meaningful relationships.

2. *Join political organisations*: Membership in political organizations and associations provides opportunities to connect with like-minded individuals, expanding the network. Attend meetings, seminars, and workshops organized by these groups to establish new contacts and learn from experienced politicians.

3. *Utilize social media*: Leverage the power of social media platforms to connect with politicians and engage with their activities. Follow influential figures, participate in discussions, and share valuable insights. Build virtual relationships that can translate into real-life connections.

4. *Attend local community events*: Strengthen political networks by engaging with the local community. Attend neighborhood meetings, volunteer for community initiatives, and participate in local events. Connecting with constituents and grassroots organizations helps establish trust, forming the foundation of a robust network.

5. *Be proactive in building relationships*: Take the initiative to reach out and connect with politicians, advisors, campaigners, and individuals actively involved in politics. Attend public forums, social gatherings, and introduce yourself. Follow up with personalized messages or emails to sustain connections.

6. *Offer support*: Reach out to fellow politicians and offer assistance whenever possible. Volunteer for campaigns, support initiatives, or promote their causes. Demonstrating commitment and support can lead to valuable alliances.

7. *Maintain regular communication*: Constantly stay in touch with contacts. Provide updates at regular intervals, share relevant information, and seek insights on important matters. Remembering birthdays, anniversaries, or other significant events contributes to maintaining thoughtful relationships.

8. *Be genuine and reliable*: Networking in politics thrives on authentic relationships built on trust and mutual

respect. Be genuine in interactions, uphold promises, and demonstrate reliability.

9. *Seek mentorship*: Identify experienced politicians who can serve as mentors and guides. Seek their advice, learn from their experiences, and build a strong professional bond. Mentorship enriches political knowledge and provides valuable connections through the mentor's network.

Networking in politics is a long-term investment that demands consistent effort, sincere intentions, and genuine interest in building meaningful connections. An individual must stay attuned to the political atmosphere and actively participate in political events to remain a significant player in the political arena.

CHAPTER 3

Crafting Persuasive Political Persona

A meticulously defined political persona serves as the linchpin for politicians to connect with their audience, promote trust, and carve a distinctive presence in politics. Understanding these fundamental elements enables politicians to effectively convey their vision, values, and policies. In politics one's image is the key to winning elections and accomplishing political objectives.

At its essence, a persona is a crafted representation or archetype of an individual's ideal self. It involves shaping a vibrant character that embodies the unique traits and aspirations of the self. This public image, carefully constructed by a politician or political figure, is presented to the public to shape perception and garner support. It encompasses how they present themselves in terms of appearance, demeanor, speeches, and overall communication style.

Establishing a personal image delves into essential questions: What does one stand for? What values are held dear? What sets an individual apart from other politicians? Answering these questions becomes the foundation for developing a unique image and persona that reflects the self. A political persona is intricately designed to align with the politician's desired image, political ideology, and targeted audience. This often involves projecting specific qualities or values, such as strength, readability, trustworthiness, or vision. Politicians strategically create and maintain their political persona to influence public opinion, attract voters, and achieve their political objectives.

Understanding the importance of persona

But why are personas crucial? Imagine attempting to sell ice to an Eskimo without understanding their preferences, lifestyle, or needs—it would be an exercise in futility! Personas empower individuals to move beyond generalized assumptions and stereotypes, allowing them to truly grasp what makes their audience tick. It is not only about policies and ideologies; it is also about the art of persuasion and connection. A captivating persona empowers politicians to efficiently communicate their ideas, connect with voters on an emotional level, and establish credibility. By embodying specific traits and values, politicians create an identity that resonates with their targeted audience, making them relatable and trustworthy.

Crafting an influential political persona is not merely a superficial endeavor; it is a strategic tool that politicians employ to steer the complex system of public opinion and political competition. It is a dynamic process that requires continuous refinement and adaptation to vibrate with evolving societal values and expectations. Ultimately, a well-crafted political persona becomes a powerful asset in the pursuit of political success and impact.

Personality Cult

A personality cult arises when a public figure, typically a political leader, is presented to the public in an idealized, heroic, and often quasi-divine manner. The phenomenon isn't unique to any one culture or historical period, appearing in various forms throughout history. It involves a deliberate and often state-supported effort to promote a leader's image, often using mass media, propaganda, and other cultural and societal channels to cultivate an image that may be largely at odds with the reality of the leader's own nature or the effects of their rule.

Historically, personality cults have been cultivated around leaders in a variety of political systems and cultural settings. Perhaps the most prominent examples in the 20th century include Joseph Stalin in the Soviet Union, Mao Zedong in China, and Adolf Hitler in Nazi Germany. Each of these leaders was portrayed as infallible and heroic, with their images ubiquitously displayed and their supposed virtues extolled through various media. In Stalin's USSR, art, literature, and music were heavily censored and shaped to glorify him and align with Soviet ideology. Mao's Cultural Revolution was marked by the omnipresent display of his quotations and images, reinforcing his god-like status in Chinese society.

Mechanisms of a Personality Cult

The construction of a personality cult typically involves several mechanisms:

1. *Media control and propaganda*: The state or movement controls the dissemination of information, ensuring that the leader is shown in a positive light. This often includes exaggeration of their achievements and suppression of information that might tarnish their image.

2. *Symbolism and iconography*: The leader's image becomes a central symbol in public spaces, homes, and workplaces, as well as in ceremonies and rituals, reinforcing their omnipresence in everyday life.

3. *Association with key values or ideologies*: The leader is portrayed as embodying the ideals of the country or the

political system, making any criticism of them equivalent to treason against the state or ideological betrayal.

4. *Cultivation of a messianic narrative:* The leader is depicted as a savior, uniquely capable of leading the nation towards a glorious future, often in times of crisis.

Formation of a Political Persona

The development of a personality cult significantly impacts the formation of a political persona by intertwining the leader's identity with the state or the political movement itself. This identity construction serves multiple strategic purposes.

Legitimacy: By cultivating an image of wisdom, strength, and paternal benevolence, the leader gains a form of legitimacy that does not depend solely on political performance or democratic processes.

Unification: A cult of personality can serve to unite the populace under a single, charismatic figure, especially in times of social unrest or political upheaval.

Suppression of dissent: The idealized image of the leader makes it difficult for opposition groups to challenge their authority without being seen as enemies of the state.

Control: By promotion an environment where questioning the leader is unthinkable, the regime can manipulate public opinion and maintains control over the society.

Implications and Consequences

While a personality cult can consolidate power and stabilize a leader's control, it also carries significant risks and negative consequences:

Distortion of reality: The glorification of a leader often involves distorting facts and history, which can lead to poor decision-making and governance based on false premises.

Suppression of individuality: In a society where a single leader's characteristics are idealized, alternative voices and identities can be marginalized or silenced, stifling creativity and diversity.

Political instability: Once the leader dies or is removed from power, the political system may become unstable without the central figure that held the cult together.

The formation of personality cult is a powerful tool for political persona construction but is fraught with moral and ethical implications. It often leads to governance that prioritizes the maintenance of an image over the pragmatic and equitable administration of the state. Furthermore, while a personality cult can temporarily provide stability and focus for a political system, it ultimately undermines the principles of democratic governance and can lead to long-term social and political problems when the cult dissolves or is dismantled. Understanding the dynamics of personality cults is crucial for recognizing the signs of authoritarian drift in political leaders and for encouragement of a more informed and resilient public.

The Political Self

The development of the "political self"—an individual's identity as it relates to politics and their understanding of their role within the political sphere—is a multifaceted process influenced by a variety of factors. These include social and familial environments, educational experiences, personal values, and significant life events. Understanding how individuals come to perceive themselves politically, form their political beliefs, and engage in political activities is essential for grasping the broader dynamics of political participation and civic engagement.

1. Family and Socialization

The family is often the first and most influential agent of political socialization. From an early age, individuals are exposed to the political opinions and behaviors of family members, which can shape their initial political orientations. This early exposures can include:

Discussion of political matters: Regular conversations that involve politics, whether about local or national issues, can stimulate an interest in political matters.

Observation of voting behaviors: Seeing family members participate in elections and other civic duties can instill similar values.

Expression of values: The expression of broader values such as fairness, justice, and community responsibility can lay the groundwork for political ideologies.

2. Education

Education plays a critical role in the development of the political self by providing knowledge about political systems, rights and responsibilities of citizenship, and the skills necessary to analyze and understand political issues. Schools often serve as a platform for the following:

Civic education: Formal education in civics, which includes understanding political structures, processes, and the importance of participation, is foundational.

Development of critical thinking: Education encourages analytical thinking, debate, and discussion, which are essential for forming independent political opinions.

Exposure to diverse viewpoints: In educational settings, individuals encounter peers and teachers with differing views, which can challenge and refine or define their political beliefs.

3. Media Influence

Media, in its various forms, significantly impacts the development of the political self by shaping perceptions of political issues and actors. It acts as a primary source of information for many, especially with the rise of digital media:

News consumption: The types of media consumed can reinforce existing beliefs or introduce new perspectives.

Social media: Platforms like X (Twitter), Facebook, and Instagram allows individuals to engage in political discourse, share opinions, and mobilize for causes, influencing political identity formation.

Selective exposure: People tend to select media sources that align with their existing beliefs, which can strengthen their political self-concept.

4. Peer Influence and Community Engagement

Interactions with peers and participation in community activities can also shape one's political self. This involves:

Discussion and debate among peers: Engaging in political conversations with friends and colleagues can influence political opinions and the sense of political efficacy.

Community involvement: Participation in local community organizations or movements can heighten political awareness and activism, reinforcing their political self.

5. Personal Experiences and Life Events

Significant personal experiences and life events can dramatically alter an individual's political self. This might include:

Economic experiences: Personal or familial economic challenges can influence political views regarding welfare, taxation, and government intervention.

Cultural encounters: Experiences with different cultures or international travel can broaden perspectives and alter political viewpoints.

Major societal events: Events such as wars, economic crises, or social movements can catalyze political involvement and shape political identities.

6. Reflective Self-Examination

As individuals mature, reflective self-examination plays an increasing role in the development of the political self. People reassess their beliefs and values in light of new information and experiences, which can lead to changes in political perspectives.

The development of the political self is a dynamic, ongoing process influenced by a complex interaction of personal experiences, social influences, and cognitive engagements. Understanding this development is crucial not only for individuals aiming to understand their own political identities but also for societies that wish to promote informed, engaged citizens.

Genetics and Social Conditioning

Yes, both genetic factors and social conditioning plays significant roles in the formation of an individual's persona. The persona, which can be understood as the outward personality or identity that a person presents to the world, is shaped by a complex interplay of inherited traits and learned behaviors influenced by the environment.

Genetic Factors

Genetics provide the biological underpinnings of our personality. Research in the field of behavioral genetics has demonstrated that many aspects of our personality, such as temperament, susceptibility to mental health disorders, and aspects of our disposition like extraversion or introversion, have a heritable component. These genetic predispositions can influence how individuals process emotions, respond to stress, and interact with their environment.

Temperament: Certain fundamental aspects of an individual's temperament, such as sensitivity to stimuli, mood stability, and adaptability, are influenced by genetic factors. These inborn traits act as a foundation upon which social experiences can build.

Neurobiology: Genetics also play a role in shaping the neurobiological processes of the brain, which affect cognitive functions and emotional regulation. For example, the balance of neurotransmitters, such as serotonin and dopamine, can affect a person's ability to experience pleasure or manage stress, influencing personality development.

Social Conditioning

While genetics set the stage, social conditioning—or the process by which individuals absorb and integrate values, norms, and behaviors from their culture and immediate environment—greatly shapes the persona. This includes the influence of family, education, social interactions, culture, and media. Social conditioning helps determine how genetic predispositions are expressed or suppressed.

Family Environment: From infancy, the family environment shapes behavior and personality through mechanisms of reinforcement, modeling, and attachment. Parenting styles, for instance, influence self-esteem, coping strategies, and social skills.

Culture and Society: Cultural norms and values significantly impact the development of persona. Culture informs our understanding of acceptable behaviors, shapes our values, and even influences our career choices and ambitions. For example, a society that values individual achievement and competitiveness might cultivate personas that are ambitious and self-reliant.

Education and Peer Interactions: Formal education and peer interactions are other major areas where social conditioning occurs. Schools teach social norms and critical thinking, while peer relationships help refine social skills and can either reinforce or challenge family and societal norms.

Interaction between Genetics and Social Conditioning

The development of persona is not simply about genetics or social environment; it is about the interaction between the two. The theory of gene-environment interaction suggests that certain environmental factors may activate or deactivate genetic predispositions. For example, a genetically predisposed resilience to stress might only become apparent in a supportive environment, or conversely, a predisposition to anxiety might not manifest unless triggered by a stressful environment.

Epigenetics: Recent advances in the field of epigenetics shows that environmental influences can affect the way genes are expressed, without altering the genetic code itself. Life experiences can lead to chemical modifications around the genes that will turn them on or off, affecting how genetic potentials are realized.

In summary, the formation of persona is a dynamic process shaped by both inherited genetic factors and social conditioning. Genetics provide the basic framework of potentialities, while social experiences mold these potentials into the persona that is presented to the world. Understanding this interaction is crucial for comprehending the full complexity of human behavior and personality development.

Building an Authentic Identity

Having an authentic political personality is not just advisable; it is crucial. Voters value honesty and transparency, making it fundamental to establish an identity that reverberates with core values and beliefs. Here are some basic strategies to build an authentic political identity:

1. *Self reflection:* This process involves introspection, where an individual looks inward to examine their thoughts, emotions, beliefs, values, and actions. Deliberate self-examination allows individuals to contemplate their experiences, analyze strengths and weaknesses, evaluate progress, and identify areas for personal growth. It furthers deeper self-awareness, helps assess goals and values, and guides conscious choices about behavior and life path. Asking introspective questions, challenging beliefs, and considering different perspectives are valuable tools for personal growth and increased self-understanding. Reflect on personal experiences that have shaped one's political ideology.

2. *Consistency:* Consistency is the quality or state of being stable and reliable. It entails coherence, harmony, or conformity in thoughts, actions, or behavior over time. Consistency in various aspects, such as logical reasoning, behavior, decision-making, and adherence to principles, is vital in personal relationships, professional settings, scientific research, and other areas where reliability and predictability are valued. Consistency in both words and actions nurtures credibility and builds trust. Public statements and positions should align with one's core values, staying true to promises made. Avoiding

flip-flopping without valid reasons is crucial to avoid appearing disingenuous.

3. *Accessibility:* Accessibility refers to the extent to which something, such as a product, service, environment, or information, is usable and understandable by a diverse range of individuals, including those with disabilities or impairments. It emphasizes removing barriers that may prevent certain individuals from fully participating in society or accessing the same opportunities as others. Accessibility covers physical, sensory, cognitive, and technological aspects to ensure inclusion and equal access for everyone. Connecting with people on a personal level, attending community events, holding town hall meetings, and actively engaging with people makes an individual relatable and approachable. Strive to be accessible as much as possible.

4. *Telling personal stories:* Share personal stories that highlights the journey and challenges overcome, confining the narrative to what is necessary. By communicating personal journey, motivations, and vision, politicians can establish an emotional connection with the electorate. The narrative should emphasize relatable experiences and challenges faced by the politician, showcasing resilience, empathy, and commitment to public service. A well-crafted personal story can evoke empathy and promote a sense of familiarity, building trust between the politician and the public.

5. *Transparency:* Transparency is the quality or state of being open, clear, and easily accessible to public scrutiny. It involves sharing information, maintaining clear communication, and being accountable for one's actions and decisions. Transparency plays a vital role in promoting trust, accountability, and informed decision-

making across different sectors and levels of society. It helps dispel doubts or suspicions. Be open about intentions, motivations, and decision-making processes.

6. *Authenticity and value:* Authenticity holds immense value, and people appreciate leaders who remain true to their beliefs, even in challenging situations. It embodies the quality of being genuine, real, and true to oneself. Authenticity entails expressing thoughts, feelings, and actions honestly and transparently, without adopting a façade or conforming to societal expectations. Often associated with sincerity, originality, and individuality, authenticity is highly valued in personal relationships, self-expression, creative endeavors, and overall well-being. Avoid adopting positions or views solely for the sake of popularity or political expediency. It is paramount for political figures to cultivate a narrative aligning with their core beliefs and values, as voters are increasingly perceptive and can easily discern insincerity or in-authenticity.

7. *Effective communication and messaging:* Politicians must master the art of persuasion, employing rhetoric and language that resonates with their target audience. Understanding demographics, cultural nuances, and electorate concerns is pivotal for tailoring messaging to their needs. Powerful speeches, articulate debates, and engaging interviews serve as avenues through which politicians can showcase their communication prowess. Delivering a clear and concise message enables politicians to inspire, motivate, and rally support from the public.

8. *Building trust and credibility:* To establish trust, politicians must demonstrate integrity, consistency, and transparency. Upholding ethical standards and fulfilling campaign promises are essential for building and maintaining credibility. A track record of integrity

and accountability strengthens the persona, instilling confidence in the electorate. Additionally, forging alliances and securing endorsements from respected figures and organizations can enhance the perceived credibility of a politician. Collaborating with experts in various fields and seeking their guidance on policy matters adds depth and substance to the persona, further establishing the politician as a trusted authority.

9. *Leveraging social media and online platform:* A robust online presence is indispensable for any politician aiming to create a convincing persona. Social media platforms provide an opportunity to connect directly with voters, disseminate information, and shape public opinion. However, striking a balance between authenticity and strategic messaging in online interactions is essential. Engaging with followers, addressing concerns, and sharing insights can humanize politicians, creating a sense of accessibility. By leveraging various digital mediums, such as videos, info-graphics, and live streams, politicians can effectively communicate their policies and initiatives, allowing voters to develop a deeper understanding of their persona.

10. *Handling public image and online presence:* Politicians must be aware of how they are portrayed in the media and take proactive steps to shape the narrative. Engaging with the press, cultivating relationships with journalists, and delivering accurate and timely information are crucial for maintaining control over public image. Moreover, a politician's physical appearance, demeanor, and body language contribute to the overall persona. Dressing appropriately, displaying confidence, and exhibiting active listening skills can positively impact public perception, reinforcing the desired image and projecting an aura of competence and leadership.

11. *Engaging with constituents:* Holding town hall meetings, attending community events, and conducting regular outreach programs allow politicians to connect with the people they represent. Actively listening to concerns, gathering feedbacks, and addressing issues demonstrate politicians' commitment to serving the community. Furthermore, incorporating grassroots campaigns and involving volunteers in the political process can strengthen the bond between the politician and constituents. This hands-on approach shows dedication, accessibility, and a genuine desire to understand and address the needs of the people, securing their identity.

12. *Managing political challenges:* Facing opposition, managing public scrutiny, and addressing controversies are inherent parts of the political journey. Handling these challenges with grace, transparency, and accountability is crucial to maintaining the integrity of the persona. Developing resilience and adaptability is essential for overcoming obstacles and turning them into opportunities for growth. Acknowledging mistakes, learning from them, and demonstrating a commitment to personal and professional development enable politicians to promote trust and strengthen their persona in the face of adversity.

Establishing political persona is a complex undertaking that demands authenticity, adept communication, trust-building, and proactive interaction with constituents. Politicians can shape a resonant persona, influencing public opinion and ensuring successful political campaigns, by recognizing the significance of personal narratives, harnessing the power of social media, and effectively navigating political challenges. Through a comprehensive and unwavering approach, politicians have the opportunity to establish themselves as trusted leaders capable of bringing about positive changes in society.

CHAPTER 4

Message Dexterity: Effective Communication

Envision a world devoid of clear communication, where ideas become tangled, and messages lose their essence in translation. In today's swiftly moving and interconnected society, the skill to articulate and convey a message with precision holds unparalleled importance.

A message, in essence, entails the process of expressing thoughts, ideas, or intentions in a lucid and succinct manner. It encompasses the art of developing a message that adeptly communicates the intended meaning to the recipient. Whether in a conversation, a written piece, or a marketing campaign, a well-defined message lays the foundation for effective communication and favorable outcomes.

A message serves as the primary instrument for establishing connections with constituents and garnering support for various ideas and policies. For individuals in positions of influence, such as politicians, the development of a well-defined message is not just important; it is a prerequisite for impactful communication and delivery, ultimately maximizing influence. Thus, the process of message drafting assumes a pivotal role in conveying information, ideas, and intentions effectively. It involves the meticulous composition, refinement, and organization of messages to ensure they possess clarity, coherence, and the desired impact.

Understanding the Term

Message dexterity refers to the art of expressing thoughts, ideas, or intentions clearly and succinctly. It is the skillful development of messages to ensure that the intended meaning reaches the audience without distortion. This skill is indispensable in diverse scenarios, be it marketing, politics, public relations, and leadership, where the ability to convey clear, persuasive, and appropriate messages is crucial.

Message dexterity is therefore not just about what is communicated, but how, when, and to whom the message is conveyed. It requires a blend of empathy, flexibility, cultural understanding, and strategic thinking. Those who master message dexterity are better positioned to influence opinions, shape perceptions, and achieve communication goals in any interactive scenario. Message dexterity is a multifaceted discipline that lies at the heart of political strategy. Effective message management can lead to a strong public image, sway public opinion, and ultimately, drive political outcomes.

Significance

Without dexterity, ideas can be misinterpreted, and the essence of communication may be lost. This underscores the need for individuals to hone their ability to create and deliver messages effectively.

It is a critical skill in today's information-saturated world, where effective communication can significantly influence outcomes across various domains such as business, politics, education, and personal relationships. The ability to adeptly fit messages to different audiences and contexts can determine the success of interactions and initiatives.

For politicians, mastering message dexterity is not just a skill; it's a necessity. The ability to articulate a clear message is paramount in garnering support, influencing opinions, and implementing policies. Politicians must meticulously draft messages that resonate with their constituents, ensuring maximum impact.

Message dexterity in politics refers to the skillful crafting and strategic delivery of messages by politicians, their advisors, and their campaigners. This skill set is crucial for shaping public opinion, influencing policy debates, and securing electoral success.

The media environment, characterized by the prevalence of social media, 24-hour news cycles, and increasingly segmented audiences, it has become more important than ever. Politicians must steer a complex array of communication channels and adapt their messages to diverse audiences who have varying interests and concerns.

Art of Persuasive Campaign Messaging

In elections, a convincing campaign message stands as the linchpin for success. The craft of constructing a message that is not only lucid and succinct but also inherently persuasive is pivotal for garnering support and rallying voters. Here are key insights and strategies for the art of crafting an impactful campaign message.

1. *Understanding the targeted audience:* Effective political messaging hinges on a fundamental principle—comprehending the targeted audience. To forge a resonating message, an in-depth understanding of their needs, concerns, and aspirations is indispensable. Robust

research, encompassing surveys, focus groups, and data analysis, provides valuable insights into demographics, values, and preferences. Segmentation of the audience based on factors such as age, gender, location, and socioeconomic status allows political communicators to develop messages effectively. This approach ensures more impactful communication by addressing specific concerns and resonating with the target audience's values and beliefs.

2. *Building an emotional connection:* Emotions play a pivotal role in motivating voters. Developing a message that taps into their emotions and values is of paramount importance. Incorporating storytelling and personal narratives that speak to the experiences and aspirations of the electorate is a key. An effective strategy involves showcasing the candidate's personal background and experiences in a relatable manner, illustrating how their journey aligns with the struggles and dreams of the voters. Sharing anecdotes and examples that highlight empathy, resilience, and a commitment to positive change humanize the candidate and bring forth emotional bonding with the audience. Beyond the candidate's story, integrating narratives of real people positively impacted or facing challenges resonates authentically with the larger community. By sharing stories of individuals and communities, the campaign demonstrates understanding and empathy for the electorate's concerns, nurturing a sense of unity and shared purpose. Drafting a message that speaks to both the heart and the mind, rooted in authenticity, empathy, and a deep understanding of the electorate's experiences and aspirations, forges a genuine and lasting connection with voters.

3. *Identifying key issues and priorities:* Determining pressing problems and important themes that resonate with the audience requires thorough research and analysis. Starting with the examination of demographic and psychographic data to understand the concerns and values of different voter groups is crucial. Political actors can conduct opinion polls, analyze social media trends, and engage in grassroots interactions with constituents. Studying past election results and relevant political trends sheds light on issues that historically sway voters. It is essential to consider both national and local issues, understanding socioeconomic, cultural, and regional dynamics. Aligning the campaign message with these findings is crucial. The message should articulate a clear vision for addressing identified issues, resonating with the values and aspirations of the electorate. Developing a narrative that speaks to the electorate's hopes, concerns, and aspirations is essential for a successful election campaign. Throughout the campaign, obtaining feedbacks and staying attuned to evolving issues and sentiments is vital to ensure the message remains relevant and resonant.

4. *Clinch to authenticity:* The message must radiate authenticity, mirroring the core values and priorities of the candidate. Avoid attempting to adopt a persona that doesn't align with the genuine self or pandering to voters. Voter discernment can detect insincerity, leading to disengagement. Authenticity in this context involves presenting the candidate, their values, and proposed policies genuinely, transparently, and in a relatable manner. Simplify language to avoid jargon or complexity, opting for a conversational tone to enhance readability. Framing techniques, such as emphasizing benefits, addressing fears, and appealing to shared values,

contribute to shaping the perception of the message, thereby increasing its effectiveness.

5. *Consistency and harmony:* Consistency and coherence form the backbone of effective political messaging. Messages should align seamlessly across various platforms and channels to uphold a unified narrative. Inconsistencies can breed confusion, undermining the credibility of the communicator. Maintain focus on the message while conveying visions and values. The candidate's public statements, actions, and policy proposals, encompassing social media posts, campaign materials, and interviews, should harmoniously align to present a cohesive and authentic identity. While addressing diverse issues, consistently tie them back to the central theme. Identifying unique selling points that differentiate from opponents and emphasizing them throughout the campaign is crucial. Developing a consistent message demands meticulous planning and coordination, nurturing the development of a strong persona and establishing trust with the audience.

6. *Strategic timing and thoughtful delivery:* Messages should be strategically delivered to maximize impact and reach the target audience when they are most receptive. Political actors must consider the political background, current events, and audience attention span when determining message timing. The effectiveness of the message is significantly influenced by its delivery. Choose the medium—speeches, press releases, social media, or traditional media—carefully based on the target audience's preferences and accessibility. For instance, younger audiences may engage more with social media, while older demographics may respond better to traditional media. Adapt the delivery to the

specific conduit to optimize impact; speeches should be eloquent and passionate, while social media posts should be concise, visually appealing, and shareable. Adapting the message to the delivery medium enhances audience attention, making it more memorable and impactful.

7. *Establishing credibility and trust:* Political figures must showcase integrity, authenticity, and a proven track record of fulfilling promises. Credibility is the linchpin; without which, the message risks skepticism or dismissal as mere rhetoric. Providing concrete evidence, statistics, and real-life examples is essential to substantiate claims and promises. Testimonials from reputable sources, experts, or individuals benefiting from proposed policies further enhance credibility. Transparency and accountability play pivotal roles in maintaining trust; any insinuation of dishonesty or evasion can tarnish the communicator's credibility, undermining the message.

8. *Adapting to evolving communication channels:* Political communication has transcended traditional outlets, demanding adaptability to the evolving scene. Political figures must take the helm of various channels effectively to reach their target audience. Social media platforms like Facebook, WhatsApp, X (Twitter), Instagram, and YouTube offer direct engagement, information sharing, and supporter mobilization opportunities. Leveraging these platforms facilitates broader outreach, especially to the younger demographic, nurturing two-way communication by addressing comments, concerns, and inquiries. Beyond social media, utilizing email newsletters, podcasts, blogs, and online forums enhances the reach and impact of political messaging. Diversifying communication channels ensures the message reaches diverse audience segments, maximizing engagement.

9. *Visual and multimedia elements:* Engaging images, videos, info-graphics, and animations serve to captivate attention, simplify complex information, and evoke emotions. Careful selection of visual elements supports the message and aligns with the target audience's aesthetics. For instance, if the message emphasizes unity and diversity, powerful images showcasing people from different backgrounds coming together can be impactful. Videos can feature personal stories, testimonials, or highlight the impact of policies on individuals and communities. Incorporating visual and multimedia elements allows political communicators to create an immersive and memorable experience, increasing the likelihood of message retention and influencing audience perceptions and actions.

10. *Repetition of messages:* Repetition is a powerful tool for reinforcing recognition among voters. Consistently repeating the message throughout the campaign, across all communications and materials, builds familiarity and reinforces key points. This strategic repetition contributes to message retention and reinforces its importance in the minds of the voters.

Developing an impactful political message demands meticulous attention to the target audience, identification of key issues, and the adept use of persuasive language and framing techniques. Consistency, timing, and delivery play pivotal roles in ensuring the message reaches the intended audience precisely when needed and through the most suitable channels. Augmenting credibility, adapting to evolving communication channels, and integrating visual and multimedia elements further amplify the influence of political messaging.

Mastering the art of drafting or developing political messages empowers political actors to effectively connect with their target audience, shape public opinion, and rally support for their cause or candidacy. Continuous analysis, adaptation, and refinement are imperative, enabling political communicators to optimize their messages and foster meaningful connections with the target audience. Developing a political message is an ongoing process necessitating constant evaluation, feedback, and adjustment.

Armed with irrefutable message and a robust ground game, one can generate momentum and attain any intended objectives. In the dynamic dominion of politics and public discourse, success hinges on perpetual evaluation, adaptation, and refinements.

CHAPTER 5

Exploring Challenges:
Navigating Political Corridors

Political choices wield considerable influence over various aspects of our lives, shaping economic policies and societal values. However, delving into the complexities of politics can seem daunting due to its convoluted and expansive nature. Attaining success in the realm of politics is a formidable task, demanding dedication, hard work, and a resolute commitment to serving the public. Nevertheless, with the right strategies and approach, one can forge a prosperous political career, effecting positive change within society. This not only facilitates informed decision-making but also establishes a connection with constituents, establishing a foundation of trust. The essence of politics—often described as the art of the possible—now requires an unprecedented level of sophistication and adaptability to manage and thrive amid these dynamics.

One of the foremost challenges in the contemporary political arena is the increased polarization of public opinion. Driven by digital echo chambers and partisan media, this polarization complicates the process of consensus-building, often stalling critical legislative actions and breeding a culture of antagonism and gridlock. Additionally, the rise of misinformation and the ease with which it spreads across social media platforms further exacerbate the difficulty of fostering informed public debates. The result is a political environment where truth and transparency are frequently overshadowed by the clamor of unverified information.

Moreover, globalization continues to reshape national politics by introducing a broader range of international factors that can influence domestic policies and political debates. From economic interdependence to environmental agreements, the decisions made within one nation can have far-reaching effects, necessitating leaders who are not only well-versed in domestic issues but are also competent in navigating international waters.

The ongoing challenges of addressing social inequality, climate change, and public health add layers of complexity to political decision-making. Each issue demands a balanced approach that considers both immediate outcomes and long-term sustainability, often requiring difficult trade-offs that can be politically contentious.

Political Acumen

Politics infiltrates every facet of society, impacting the laws governing us, the quality of public services, and the allocation of resources. Lacking a comprehensive understanding of political matters puts individuals at risk of becoming passive recipients of decisions rather than active participants. To actively contribute to shaping the future of their communities and nations, citizens must grasp the niceties of political systems and comprehend the ramifications of diverse policy choices.

Informed Decision-Making: A robust grasp of politics empowers individuals to make informed decisions about their lives and society. It provides insight into government functionality, the repercussions of political actions, and the impact of politics.

Political awareness enables individuals to vote judiciously, support candidates and policies aligning with their values, and actively participate in the democratic process.

Effective Citizenship: Political understanding is foundational to being an engaged and responsible citizen. It equips citizens to actively participate in public affairs, express their opinions, and hold elected representatives accountable. Without political knowledge, individuals may struggle to contribute or advocate for their rights.

Policy Influence: Political literacy enables individuals to shape policies addressing societal issues. Understanding political systems and policy formation processes allows citizens to advocate for changes, participate in public debates, and influence legislation. Political awareness provides individuals with tools to steer the trajectory of their society.

Social Cohesion: Political understanding promotes social cohesion by bringing forth dialogue, comprehension, and compromise. It allows individuals to engage with diverse perspectives, bridging ideological gaps. Understanding political systems and ideologies can overcome prejudice, reduce polarization, and create opportunities for constructive conversations and cooperation.

Awareness of Power Dynamics: Politics revolves around power distribution in society. Understanding these processes helps individuals recognize power patterns, identify inequalities, and challenge oppressive systems. It allows people to question authority, demand accountability, and advocate for social justice.

Protection of Rights and Freedom: Politics directly impacts the protection of individual rights and freedoms. Through an understanding of political systems, citizens can identify potential threats to their rights, recognize attempts to undermine democratic principles, and actively safeguard their liberties.

A lack of political understanding can leave individuals vulnerable to manipulation or the erosion of their rights.

Building a Foundation

Every successful structure relies on a sturdy foundation, and individuals aspiring to be well-informed and engaged citizens are no exception. In politics, establishing a robust groundwork entails gaining knowledge about diverse political systems, ideologies, institutions, and the processes shaping societies.

Explore Political Systems and ideologies: To comprehend political issues effectively, it is essential to begin by delving into various political systems and their core principles. This involves understanding democracy, authoritarianism, socialism, and other governance forms. It also entails knowledge of how laws are formulated, the roles of executive, legislative, and judicial branches, and the functions of local, national, and international bodies. Analyzing the strengths and weaknesses of different systems offers valuable insights into the exercise of political power and its consequences. Political ideologies serve as a framework for grasping the values, beliefs, and goals behind political movements. From liberalism to conservatism, socialism to libertarianism, each ideology presents distinct perspectives on government roles, individual rights, and wealth distribution. Familiarizing oneself with these ideologies enhances comprehension of political debates and policy choices.

Examining Historical Context: Deepening our understanding of political systems involves examining historical events and their impact on societies. Analyzing major political movements, revolutions, and the development of key institutions helps recognize patterns, gain insights, and understand the evolution of political systems over time.

Cultivating Critical Thinking: Practical critical thinking skills are essential for evaluating political information and arguments. Analyzing sources for credibility, bias, and logical consistency, questioning assumptions, seeking evidence, and making informed judgments help steer complex political discourse and distinguish fact from opinion.

Keep Abreast of Current Events: Staying informed about domestic and international political developments through reputable news outlets and diverse perspectives aids in understanding different angles of a story. Engaging with current events provides insights into how political decisions are made, their societal impact, and how various actors shape the political landscape.

Active Participation: Involvement in civic activities, such as joining local community organizations, attending town hall meetings, or participating in political campaigns, offers firsthand experience and insights into political processes. Active involvement allows individuals to witness how politics operates on the ground and help for a deeper understanding of the issues at stake.

Foster Discussion and Debate: Engaging in respectful discussions and debates with individuals holding different political views, refines arguments, provides new insights, and develops empathy for diverse opinions. Constructive dialogue is crucial for cultivating a nuanced political understanding and promoting democratic values.

Education on Global Affairs: Understanding international relations, global governance, and the interconnectedness of political systems worldwide is vital for developing a holistic political perspective.

Ethical and Moral Considerations: Reflecting on the ethical and moral dimensions of political choices, policies, and actions helps individuals develop a well-rounded political understanding that considers broader societal impacts and ethical responsibilities.

Informed Citizenship

Understanding politics holds immense importance for various reasons. It lays the groundwork for a comprehensive grasp of the political background, empowering citizens to make well-informed decisions. Here are key strategies for staying informed in an age of information overload.

Diversifying Information Sources

In an age overwhelmed with information, it is imperative to draw knowledge from a multitude of sources to gain a holistic insight into political matters. Relying solely on one news outlet may result in biased perspectives or incomplete coverage. Employing diverse sources like reputable newspapers, online platforms, and podcasts allows individuals to access varying viewpoints, shaping more nuanced opinions. Subscribing to digital news platforms offering in-depth analyses and investigative reporting further enhances awareness.

Fact-Checking and Media Literacy

Given the surge in "fake news" and misinformation, honing media literacy skills is paramount. Fact-checking claims, verifying sources, and critically evaluating information can help separate facts from fiction. Fact-checking organizations and credible news outlets serve as valuable resources in gauging the accuracy and credibility of news stories. Vigilance against misinformation and disinformation campaigns, designed to manipulate public opinion, is crucial. Seek reputable sources adhering to journalistic standards, citing their sources, and providing evidence-based reporting.

In-depth Reading

Beyond news articles, delving into books, essays, and long-form journalism adds depth to understanding convoluted political issues. These sources offer detailed analyses and historical context, contributing to a more comprehensive comprehension of political dynamics.

Active Participation in Civil and Political Discourses

Staying informed transcends passive consumption; it involves actively engaging in civil discourse. Participating in respectful discussions, attending community forums, and joining political debates broaden perspectives and offer a deeper understanding of various viewpoints. Prioritize respectful communication and active listening when involved in political discussions. Being open to alternative viewpoints enhances comprehension of complex issues.

Approach the topic with an open mind, seeking diverse perspectives, and challenging personal beliefs. Maintain curiosity, ask questions, and take a proactive stance in seeking reliable and accurate information. Staying abreast of current affairs is not just a responsibility; it is a continuous journey towards a well-informed and engaged citizenry.

The Influence of Technology on Political Dynamics

Technology serves as a gateway to a wealth of information, encompassing news, analyses, and research on political issues and developments. It facilitates direct participation in political processes through platforms like social media, where individuals can engage in discussions, debate political matters, connect with elected officials, and organize advocacy efforts. Technological tools, such as data visualization and analytics, play a vital role in demystifying intricate political trends and patterns, making it more accessible for people to comprehend and interpret political events.

Social Media and Citizen Journalism

The rise of social media has revolutionized the dissemination and consumption of information. While social media platforms offer increased accessibility to news and diverse perspectives, they also present challenges due to the proliferation of misinformation and the creation of echo chambers. Combining social media usage with critical thinking and fact-checking skills empowers individuals to understand this digital domain effectively.

Online Political Resources

The internet serves as a vast resource for those seeking to grasp political issues. Websites, blogs, and online forums dedicated to politics provide in-depth analyses, research papers, and expert opinions. Engaging with reputable online political resources enhances knowledge and nurtures a more comprehensive understanding of complex political topics. Consider exploring academic journals, policy think tanks, and research institutes that publish studies on political issues, offering valuable insights backed by rigorous research and analysis.

Exploring Political Ideologies

Understanding political ideologies is pivotal in shaping policy debates. Liberalism emphasizes individual freedoms and limited government intervention, while conservatism leans towards tradition and the preservation of existing structures. Socialism advocates for social equality and collective ownership, while libertarianism focuses on individual liberty and limited state intervention.

Technology's role in politics is multifaceted, providing access to information, enabling engagement, and offering tools for analysis. It is essential for individuals to discover this digital field with discernment, combining technological resources with critical thinking to foster a more informed and participatory citizenry.

Building a Research Team for Informed Decision-Making

Consider hiring a research team to be on the right track on important issues particularly, if time is of the essence. Here's why bringing a research team on board is essential:

Expertise and diverse perspectives: A research team consists of individuals with diverse backgrounds, expertise, and perspectives. This diversity enables comprehensive analysis, interpretation, and evaluation of political phenomena from multiple angles, ensuring a holistic understanding.

Rigorous research methods: Research teams are well-versed in employing rigorous research methodologies. They conduct in-depth investigations, collect and analyse data, study existing literature, and develop empirical informed theories. By utilizing robust research methods, they contribute to the generation of reliable and valid knowledge about political phenomena.

Informed policy recommendations: A research team's findings often serve as the foundation for policy recommendations. By thoroughly examining political issues, they identify potential solutions, propose policy alternatives, and inform decision-makers about the implications of different policy choices. Their research helps shape informed policy decisions that are grounded in evidence.

Identifying trends and patterns: Political understanding rests upon recognizing trends, patterns, and underlying factors that shape political events. Research teams are adept at identifying these trends by examining historical data, cross-national comparison, and longitudinal studies. They help uncover long-term patterns and contribute to a deeper understanding of political processes.

Filling knowledge gaps: Political phenomena are complex and multifaceted, often requiring expertise across various disciplines. Research team helps bridge knowledge gaps by polling together expertise from diverse field such as political science, sociology, economics, and history.

Addressing knowledge deficits: Research teams actively work towards overcoming knowledge deficits by conducting empirical studies to answer pressing political questions. They explore uncharted territories, delve into overlooked issues, and contribute new insights to the field. This pursuit of knowledge helps advance political understanding.

Collaboration and peer review: Research team often engage in collaboration and undergo rigorous peer review processes. By working together and subjecting their research to critical evaluation, they ensure the quality and accuracy of their findings. This scrutiny strengthens the reliability and overall credibility of their work.

Briefings and meetings (BAM)

Make time for briefings and meetings with experts, lobbyists, and other stakeholders to gain insights and perspectives on specific issues. This can be particularly helpful if an individual is working on legislation or policy initiatives. In addition to attending town hall and community meetings, politicians should also make an effort to meet with constituents one-on-one. This can include holding office hours or scheduling meetings with community leaders. By meeting with constituents, politicians can better understand their concerns and build relationships that will help them serve their communities more effectively.

Information exchange: BAM provide a platform for the exchange of relevant information among the political actors. This could include updates on policy developments, intelligence briefings, economic data, and other critical information. By sharing and discussing information, participants gain a comprehensive understanding of the politics and can make informed decisions.

Policy formulation: Through BAM, policy makers can discuss and collaborate on policy formulation. These interaction allows different perspectives to be shared, enabling a more potential policy impacts, alternatives, and trade-offs. By engaging in collaborative discussions, policymakers enhance their understanding of complex issues and can make better-informed decisions.

Coordination and consensus-building: BAM bring together key stakeholders, such as politicians, government officials, and experts, to coordinate their efforts and forge consensus. Political understanding is deepened when diverse viewpoints are heard, debated and refined. Consensus-building ensures that decisions are grounded in a broader understanding of various perspectives and increases the chance of successful implementation.

Accountability and transparency: BAM uphold principles of accountability and transparency in politics. They provide opportunities for politicians to justify their decisions explain their actions and answer questions from colleagues, the media and the public. This promotes greater understanding of political intentions, enhances trust, and allows for critical examination and appraisal of policies.

Networking and relationship building: Political understanding relies on effective networking and relationship building. BAM offer opportunities for politicians and other officials to connect with each other build relationships and establish personal rapport. These networks cultivate better collaboration, trust and communication among political actors, leading to improved political understanding and cooperation.

Public engagement: BAM can also contribute to political understanding by including representatives from civil societies, academia, and other interest groups. By engaging broader range of perspectives, policy makers gain insights, expertise and public feedbacks, leading to more informed and efficient decision-making processes and therefore attend BAM as much as possible.

Staying informed and up-to-date is essential for success as a politician. By utilizing a range of strategies, including reading widely, attending events, networking, utilizing social media, conducting research, hiring a research team, and attending briefings, political actors can stay informed and make informed decisions that benefit their constituents and the community.

CHAPTER 6

Fundraising:
Effective Fundraising Strategies

Fundraising is the process of gathering voluntary contributions or financial support from individuals, organisations, or the community for a specific cause or project. It is an essential activity conducted by non-profit organisations, charities, school, political campaigns, and various other entities to generate funds to support their activities, initiatives or goals.

Fundraising encompasses the strategic development and execution of plans to attract and persuade potential donors, fostering financial contributions. Diverse approaches are employed in this endeavor, ranging from individual solicitations and organizational fundraising events to seeking corporate sponsorships, applying for grants, conducting online crowd funding campaigns, and engaging in partnerships and collaborations.

The fund raised through these efforts is used to support specific causes or projects such as financing research and development, supporting humanitarian aid efforts, funding education programmes, promoting social causes, assisting disaster relief efforts, or financing artistic and cultural events, among others.

Effective fundraising lies in the cultivation of relationships with potential donors, adept communication of the mission and impact of the organization or cause, and the demonstration of transparency and accountability in fund utilization. Successful fundraisers employ an array of strategies, including donor recognition programs, personalized appeals, storytelling, networking, and leveraging social media platforms to engage and attract individuals.

In the dominion of political endeavors, effective fundraising and budgeting emerge as critical components for success. A stout financial foundation is imperative to build a campaign infrastructure, engage with voters, and compete with other candidates. The piece underscores the significance of implementing the right strategies and tactics to establish a formidable finance operation that supports a candidate's political ambitions.

Fundraising and Budgeting

Fundraising serves as the lifeblood that empowers candidates to impel the convoluted setting of elections effectively.

A. Understanding the power of Fundraising

The power of financial resources: Raising ample funds is pivotal for running campaigns seamlessly. It fuels essential operations such as hiring dedicated staff, securing campaign offices, investing in advertising across diverse channels, conducting insightful market research, and orchestrating well-planned events. The goal is clear – to execute strategies with precision, leaving a lasting impact on the audience. Financial resources allow us to invest in various channels such as digital marketing, print media, social media advertising, and event sponsorships.

Establishing credibility and trust: A well-funded campaign not only speaks volumes about credibility but also radiates professionalism. When potential supporters see the necessary resources to back our message, they are more likely to trust and engage with our campaign. Fundraising allows us to demonstrate our commitment, dedication, and ability to deliver on the promises made. Transparency and ethics play a crucial role here; adhering to campaign finance laws, coupled with honesty about fundraising and spending practices, strengthens the foundation of trust.

Message amplification: Campaign funds, garnered through contributions, become a potent tool for amplifying messages. Whether through traditional media like television and radio or modern channels like online advertisements and social media promotions, candidates can consistently disseminate their messages. This strategic dissemination aids in building name recognition, shaping public opinion, and cultivating a positive image.

Voter outreach: Running a successful campaign requires reaching out to voters at various stages of the election cycle. Fundraising facilitates voter outreach efforts such as door-to-door canvassing, phone banking, organizing rallies and town hall meetings, hosting fundraisers, and engaging with supporters through digital platforms. These activities help candidates connect with voters, build relationships, and gain support.

Competitive advantage: In competitive political races, substantial funding becomes a game-changer. Well-funded campaigns can invest in sophisticated data analytics, professional consulting services and advanced technologies, allowing them to target specific voter demographics, prioritise outreach efforts and make informed strategic decisions. This competitive edge can help candidates gain an upper hand over their opponents.

Flexibility and adaptability: Political campaigns are dynamic by nature, requiring the ability to adapt to changing circumstances, respond to opponents, and take advantage of emerging opportunities. Strong fundraising allows campaigns to be flexible, adjust strategies, allocate resources to priority areas, and seize strategic moments, such as responding to opposition attacks or capitalizing on favourable news cycles.

B. Fund Raising Methods and Strategies

Developing a robust finance plan: A comprehensive finance plan is essential to guide the fundraising efforts. This plan should meticulously outlines the campaign's expenses and revenue sources, a timeline for fundraising activities, and a donor list that identifies potential supporters. Such a plan facilitates expense tracking, manage resources effectively, and make strategic decisions to allocate resources. The budget should include a detailed breakdown of all the expenses, including staffing, advertising, travel, and other campaign-related costs.

Harnessing individual donations: Among the most common and effective fundraising methods is soliciting individual donations. This approach involves reaching out to potential supporters, explaining the campaign's mission and goals, and encouraging them to contribute financially. Employ diverse channels like personalized emails, social media campaigns, and direct mail to reach a wider audience and enhance the likelihood of securing donations.

Corporate sponsorships: Collaborating with corporations and businesses can provide a significant boost to the fundraising efforts. Seek out companies that side with the campaign's values and objectives, and propose mutually beneficial partnerships.

Corporate sponsorships can come in the form of financial contributions, in-kind donations, or event sponsorships.

Crowd funding: In recent years, crowd funding has gained immense popularity as a fundraising method. Online platforms offer avenues to mobilise campaigns and reach vast audiences. Develop a persuasive story, showcase the impact and intend of the campaign, and offer incentives to encourage individuals to contribute.

Grant funding: Exploring grant opportunities are another viable option. Research and identify foundations, organizations, and government programs that provide grants for projects associated with the campaign's mission. Make a strong grant proposal highlighting the campaign's goals, expected outcomes, and the impact it will have on the community.

Leverage Technology: Technology proves to be a potent fundraising tool. Consider using online platforms to accept donations and reach a broader audience. Social media can also be an effective way to engage with supporters and share updates about the campaign.

Host Events: Events can be a great way to build relationships with supporters and raise funds. Consider hosting events like fundraisers, meet-and-greets, and town hall and community meetings to engage with voters and donors. Events are an effective ways to engage potential donors and generate funds. Consider hosting charity galas, benefit concerts, or community gatherings that ally with the campaign's mission. These events not only provide an opportunity to raise funds but also serve as platforms for creating awareness and building relationships.

Target Major Donors: Major donors can exert a substantial influence on the campaign. Develop a strategy for identifying and engaging with potential major donors, and be prepared to make a strong case for why they should support a particular candidacy.

Build a Strong Volunteer Network: Volunteers are valuable resource for fundraising. Encourage volunteers to reach out to their personal networks and ask for donations on our campaign's behalf. Train them and make them move.

C. Planning and Executing a Fundraising Campaign

Setting clear and measurable goals: Before initiating any fundraising campaign, it is imperative to establish clear and measurable objectives. This may include pinpointing specific fundraising targets, such as a total fundraising goal or a goal for a particular quarter or fundraising events. Determine the specific financial target aimed to achieve and outline how these funds will be allocated to support the campaign activities. Establishing a budget and timeline aids in organization and progress tracking.

Engage and Mobilize Supporters: A successful fundraising campaign relies on the support of individuals who reverberate with a common cause. Engage the supporters through various channels, such as social media, email newsletters, and in-person events. Create convincing content that showcases the impact of their contributions and encourages them to spread the word.

Build Strategic Partnerships: Collaborating with like-minded organizations and influencers can significantly enhance the fundraising campaign. Seek partnerships with local nonprofits, community groups, and influential individuals who share similar goals or target similar audiences. By combining resources, message can be amplified, reach new supporters, and expand the fundraising potential.

Provide Incentives: To boost donations, consider offering perks or rewards to contributors. These can range from exclusive merchandise, personalized thank-you notes, or invitations to campaign-related events. Providing incentives not only encourages individuals to donate but also fosters a sense of appreciation and loyalty among the supporters.

D. Analyzing Fundraising Performance

Data tracking and Analysis: Optimizing any fundraising effort requires meticulous tracking and analysis of relevant data. Implement strong analytics tools to measure the success of different fundraising channels, campaigns, and donation sources. This data will help to identify areas of improvement, refining strategies, and make data-driven decisions to maximize the campaign's impact.

Donor Relationship Management: Building and maintaining strong relationships with the donors is essential for long-term fundraising success. Implement a donor relationship management system to track donor interactions, personalize communications, and express gratitude for their support. Regularly update those donors on the progress and impact of the campaign to foster a sense of ownership and engagement.

Continuous Optimization: Fundraising campaigns require ongoing optimization and adaptation. Regularly review the fundraising strategies, evaluate their effectiveness, and make necessary adjustments. Experiment with different messaging, donation amounts, and fundraising methods to identify the most successful approaches for the campaign. Identify what is working well and what can be improved, and iterate the approach accordingly.

Donor Recognition: Publicly recognize and appreciate the donors through social media shout-outs, donor spotlights, or naming opportunities. Highlight their generosity and demonstrate the collective efforts behind the campaign's success.

A well-executed fundraising plan, incorporating clear objectives, supporter engagement, strategic partnerships, and effective performance analysis, establishes a solid foundation for a successful campaign. The continual optimization of strategies and thoughtful donor recognition further contribute to building a lasting and impactful fundraising initiative.

Fundraising to establish a stout campaign necessitates a strategic approach, detailed planning, and committed execution. Utilizing diverse fundraising methods, including individual donations, corporate sponsorships, crowd funding, and grant funding, enables the acquisition of essential financial resources to propel any campaign forward. A key to maximizing the impact of fundraising efforts is the active engagement and stewardship of donors, meticulous data tracking, and continuous optimization of strategies. It is crucial to note that a good message alone is not sufficient for a strong campaign; the support of a vibrant and dedicated community is equally vital. With a well-executed fundraising plan, one can lay a sturdy foundation for a successful campaign that instigates lasting change.

CHAPTER 7

Building Support:
Importance of Grassroots Organizing

Establishing a formidable grassroots movement stands as a pivotal factor in achieving success. The essence of grassroots activism lies in mobilizing individuals at the local level, instigating change, swaying public opinion, and influencing policy decisions.

In politics, the term "grassroots" denotes a movement or activity that originates and gains strength from the ordinary people at the local level. It emphasizes the involvement and participation of individuals within a community, rather than relying solely on established political institutions or higher levels of authority.

The term "grassroots" implies a bottom-up approach, where change and influence starts at the local level and gradually work their way up to influence higher levels of government or institutions. Grassroots movements are typically characterized by their decentralized nature, relying on the collective power of individuals rather than top-down directives.

Grassroots politics places a distinct focus on addressing the concerns, needs, and opinions of everyday citizens, with the primary goal of empowering them and providing a voice in decision-making processes. This often entails the organization and mobilization of individuals to champion specific causes, partake in community initiatives, or lend support to particular candidates for public office.

In essence, grassroots politics embodies the belief that ordinary individuals, through their active engagement and collaboration, wield substantial influence in shaping policies, steering public opinion, and catalyzing social and political transformation. While fundraising remains an indispensable component of any political campaign, concurrently establishing a strong base of support among constituents becomes equally imperative.

Grassroots organizing emerges as a highly effective strategy for building a community of dedicated supporters committed to propagating messages to a broader audience. In doing so, it creates a ripple effect, amplifying impact and cultivating a sense of collective responsibility in the pursuit of shared goals. It is not merely a strategic maneuver but a dynamic force capable of reshaping the narrative and direction of political landscapes.

Grassroots involvement: Its indispensability

Representation: Grassroots movements serve as a vehicle for a more diverse range of voices and perspectives to be acknowledged. These initiatives provide an avenue for ordinary citizens, who may lack positions of power, to actively participate in the political process. By amplifying the concerns of marginalized communities, grassroots movements ensure their interests are considered in policy-making.

Democratic participation: Grassroots involvement nurture a more participatory and inclusive democracy. By engaging citizens at the local level, grassroots movements encourage people to actively contribute to political decision-making rather than being passive observers. This helps to strengthen the democratic fabric of a society and enhance civic engagement.

Accountability: Grassroots movements serve as a check on political power. When citizens organize at the grassroot level, they can hold elected officials accountable for their actions and advocate for policies that ally with the interests and values of their communities. Grassroots campaigns can influence the political agenda, push for reforms, and challenge established power structures.

Building momentum: Grassroots movements possess the potential to generate significant momentum over time. By starting small and gradually expanding their reach, these movements can attract more supporters, gain media attention, and ultimately impact public opinion and electoral outcomes.

Driving policy change: Throughout history, grassroots activism has played a crucial role in driving policy. By organizing and advocating for specific policy reforms, grassroots movements can put pressure on lawmakers, government agencies, and other decision-makers to address important issues.

Bottom-up policy development: Grassroots movements often draw attention to issues that may not receive adequate consideration within the mainstream political discourse. By organizing at the local level, citizens can identify and address community-specific problems and propose innovative solutions. Grassroots initiatives can influence policy development from the bottom-up, ensuring that policies are responsive to the real needs of the people.

Amplifying voices: Grassroots movements provide a platform for those who feel marginalized by the political establishment. They provide a platform for individuals to express their concerns, opinions, and ideas, which can influence policy decisions and shape the overall political discourse.

Mobilizing collective action: Grassroots movements have the potential to mobilize large numbers of people around shared causes or goals. Harnessing the collective power of individuals through protests, campaigns, or community organizing, these efforts create momentum and build public support for political initiatives, increasing the likelihood of success.

Overall, grassroots involvement in politics is essential for nurturing a more inclusive, participatory, and responsive political system. It empowers ordinary citizens, amplifies diverse voices, holds leaders accountable, drives policy development, and mobilizes collective action for positive change.

Understanding Grassroots Activism

Grassroots activism embodies the collaborative endeavors of individuals profoundly dedicated to a specific political cause or campaign. Diverging from conventional top-down methodologies, grassroots movements initiate at the local level, steadily amassing influence and ultimately shaping broader political territory. This bottom-up approach hinges on harnessing the power of the people to instigate change. Fundamentally, grassroots activism seeks to empower individuals and communities, affording them a voice and the capacity to enact meaningful change. In contrast to reliance on established political institutions or traditional power hierarchies, grassroots activism underscores the potency of collective action and mobilization.

Grassroots activists often coalesce into diverse entities, such as community organizations, non-profit groups, or social movements. Engaging in activities like public demonstrations, protests, lobbying, direct action, and community outreach, they aim to raise awareness, galvanize support, and exert pressure on policymakers to address their concerns.

The efficacy of grassroots activism lies in its aptitude for connecting with people on a local level, where the impacts of political decisions are keenly felt. By bringing in community solidarity and championing issue-based advocacy, grassroots activists draw attention to social injustices, advocate for policy reforms, and amplify the voices of marginalized groups that might otherwise be overlooked.

Throughout history, grassroots activism has played a pivotal role in shaping movements, driving social change, and influencing policy agendas. Examples include the civil rights movement in the United States, anti-apartheid struggles in South Africa, and the environmental movement advocating for climate change awareness.

In contemporary politics, grassroots activism continues to exert significant influence. Through the use of social media, digital platforms, and on-the-ground organizing, activists can rapidly share information, build networks, and mobilize supporters. Overall, it stands as a vital component of democratic societies, empowering citizens to actively engage in shaping political processes and holding their representatives accountable. It serves as a formidable tool to challenge the status quo, address systemic inequalities, and advocate for a more inclusive and responsive political system.

Building Strong Ground Game

The significance of a vigorous ground game cannot be overstated when it comes to securing victories in elections. This multifaceted approach involves the meticulous organization and mobilization of supporters with the goal of reaching voters and persuading them to rally behind a candidate. In closely contested elections, a well-executed ground game can prove to be the decisive factor between triumph and defeat. To ensure success, it is imperative to formulate a comprehensive outreach plan encompassing a diverse array of tactics and strategies designed to effectively engage with voters.

Building a strong foundation for grassroots organizing and voter outreach is pivotal. This strategic approach not only facilitates the creation of a dedicated network of supporters but also empowers the campaign to mobilize this support base to actively participate in the electoral process. The ultimate aim is to secure a high voter turnout, translating into success on the crucial Election Day.

Strategies and Action plans

Defining goals: Clearly outline the objectives of the grassroots efforts, whether it is raising awareness, garnering support for a cause, or advocating a specific policy. Define goals precisely to maximize focus and efforts. Clear intentions enable ongoing progress evaluation.

Developing voter contact plan: A comprehensive voter contact plan is essential to guide ground game efforts. This plan should include a timeline for door-to-door canvassing, phone banking, and other outreach activities. Coordinate with fellow supporters, family members, friends, party workers, and well wishers while developing the plan.

Identify relevant issues: Unite people effectively by identifying common issues. However, there are also issues that are specific to certain areas or region that are more pressing needing immediate attention. Identify issues and recognize the demands of the specific areas or people and work out specific plans to address it.

Identify targeted audience: Identify the specific audience to engage with; Political actors or influencers, contractors, organisation leaders, elders, party members, old supporters, new supporters, well-wishers, technocrats, bureaucrats, opponents. Setting up and identifying the target audience will enable to make a more finite and workable message to deliver. There is also a need to identify the needs, attitude and aspiration of the area under consideration for visitation and campaign so that a specific need based policies can be formulated.

Building trust: Prioritize trust-building over mere professionalism. Engage with voters by listening to their concerns, sharing values, and responding genuinely to their needs. Maintain respect, empathy, and honesty in interactions, avoiding divisive language for a fruitful and enduring. And do not lie under any circumstances.

Recruiting and training volunteers: Volunteers are the backbone of any successful ground game. Recruit and train volunteers to reach voters and share the intended message effectively. Volunteers are valuable resource for election campaign, helping with everything from canvassing and phone banking to organizing events and fundraisers. Provide adequate training to the volunteers and recognize their contributions towards the campaign.

Build a network, collaborate and form alliance: Form a network of like-minded individuals who share similar passion for the cause. Reach out to friends, family, colleagues, and community leaders who may be interested in joining the campaign movement. Pull social media platforms, community events, and online forums to connect with potential supporters. Collaborate with other grassroots organizations, advocacy groups, and political influencers who share similar goals. By forming alliances, and combining resources, it will amplify collective impact.

Develop a strong message: Draft a gripping message that communicates the importance of the cause and which reflects the prime motive of the campaign. The message should be clear, concise, and emotionally engaging, inspiring people to take action and join the movement. Any message which does not trigger the mind will not be impactful. Message should be developed according to the understanding level of the audience for a meaningful delivery and finest impact.

Organize events and actions: Organize impactful local events, rallies, and actions to mobilize supporters and raise awareness about the cause. Utilize social media platforms, email campaigns, and traditional media outlets to promote events and attract a wider audience. Once potential supporters are identified, it is important to engage with them significantly. This can include holding community events, door-to-door canvassing, or hosting town hall meetings to discuss issues that are important to the constituents. This will create a strong relationship with them and evolve a sense of community feeling around the campaign.

Harness technology: Technology can be a valuable tool for organizing and mobilizing supporters. Consider using online tools like peer-to-peer texting and social media to reach voters and encourage engagement. This can include using platforms such as Facebook, Instagram, Whatsapp and X (Twitter) to share updates and engaging with supporters as well as creating a campaign website to provide information about upcoming events.

Community engagement: Engage with the local community by attending town hall meetings, speaking at public forums, and collaborating with other grassroots organizations. Establishing connections and building relationships within the community will strengthen the movement's credibility and broaden its impact. Make them feel your prominence and concern by initiating need based activities and orient them with responsibilities associated with it. Coordinate activities with the local leaders for maximum impact.

Dynamic monitoring and adjustment: Continuously monitor and adjust the ground game strategy throughout the campaign to stay adaptable in changing circumstances. A game plan dynamics should be flexible enough to suit with any given circumstances because static approach in politics is always dangerous. What plan works and what does not, is an assignment of the field director. And anything that does not work well has to change or done away with altogether.

Supporting party workers: Most of the time, politics are played on the party lines and therefore, party workers should not be neglected at any cost. Party workers at the grassroots should be respected at all times. The grassroots leaders are the first line to address the concerns and issue of the people therefore develop leadership at the grassroots to address the issues and to further the agendas of the campaign.

Acknowledging loyalists: Never overlook the contributions of loyalists who have steadfastly supported the campaign. Provide due recognition and acknowledgments to these committed individuals whose unwavering support has been a constant. Nurturing this dedicated category can yield significant positive outcomes and contribute to the campaign's success.

Grassroots activism holds significance as it empowers ordinary individuals to actively engage in the democratic process, exert influence on social and political transformations, and amplify awareness on critical issues such as environmental justice, human rights, and public health. By rallying communities behind shared objectives, it becomes a catalyst for meaningful change. This form of activism wields substantial influence over policies and institutions, particularly impacting the lives of marginalized or oppressed individuals. Serving as a potent tool for advancing social justice and democracy, grassroots activism welcomes participation from everyone. It is precisely for these reasons that establishing a strong foundation at the grassroots level becomes an essential undertaking for political campaigns.

CHAPTER 8

Public Speaking: Delivering Confident and Authoritative Speeches

Public speaking, a dynamic art form, requires finesse and mastery. Public speaking is more than mere words; it's an act of connecting with a live audience. It involves communicating information, ideas, or opinions in a clear and effective manner in front of a group of people. Public speaking can take place in various settings, such as conferences, meetings, classrooms, or public events. It is a structured, deliberate, and prepared way of expressing a message, idea, opinion, concept, principle, or belief that is intended to inform, entertain, or persuade the listeners. It can be done in person or through digital technology, and may use visual or audio aids to enhance the oral communication.

The primary goal of public speaking is to inform, persuade, entertain, or inspire the audience. It requires the speaker to organize their thoughts, develop a coherent message, and deliver it confidently and convincingly.

Public speaking is a daunting task, but it is an essential skill for many professionals, including politicians. Whether delivering a speech, participating in a debate, or engaging with constituents, effective public speaking can help connect with audience and convey message with clarity and impact.

Types of public speaking

One prevalent form is informative speaking, where the primary goal is to share knowledge on a particular subject. This type of presentation is commonly integrated into different professions. For instance, physicians often lecture about their areas of expertise to medical students, fellow physicians, and patients. Teachers frequently find themselves presenting to both parents and students. Even firefighters give demonstrations on effectively controlling house fires. Informative speaking is a fundamental aspect of numerous occupations and daily activities, making effective communication a vital skill in today's world.

Another common motive for addressing an audience is persuasion. In our daily lives, we frequently need to convince, motivate, or persuade others to alter their beliefs, take action, or reconsider a decision. Elected officials, in particular, rely heavily on persuasive speeches for career success. Whether public speaking is a regular occurrence or a sporadic event, persuading others is a challenging but rewarding task when honed as a skill.

Entertaining speaking encompasses a wide range of occasions, including introductions, wedding toasts, award presentations, eulogies at funerals, after-dinner speeches, and motivational speeches. Dating back to the ancient Greeks, Aristotle identified epideictic speaking (speaking in a ceremonial context) as a significant form of address. Similar to persuasive and informative speaking, there are professionals, ranging from religious leaders to comedians, who earn a living solely from delivering entertaining speeches. As anyone who has watched an awards show on television or witnessed an unprepared best man deliver a wedding toast can attest, speaking to entertain demands thorough preparation and practice to be effective.

Tips and techniques for public speaking

Confidence and authority: When confidence is projected, audiences are captivated, their trust is gained and the credibility of the speaker is established. Authority, on the other hand, reflects proficiency, knowledge, and command over the subject matter. By embodying confidence and authority, message can be conveyed effectively, actions are inspired and thus leaving a lasting impression. An individual can have confidence if he has authority over the subject matter.

Resilient mindset: Public speaking often triggers fear and nervousness. Developing a strong mindset involves reframing thoughts to focus on the positive aspects of speaking engagements. Clinch the opportunity to share and connect with the audience, rather than dwelling on potential mistakes or judgment.

Understanding the audience: Knowing the audience is important. Understand the needs, interests, demographics, interests, and knowledge level and expectations of the audience to mold the message accordingly. This includes understanding their interests, values, and concerns. Messages should connect to the audience for more effective and productive outcome. Customize the content and delivery to resonate with their needs and expectations.

Developing engaging presentations: Prepare the message well in advance. Adequate preparation is vital for boosting confidence and authority. Relevant data should be extremely researched and organized. A well-prepared speaker will speak with authority and respond to audience queries with confidence. This includes identifying key points, supporting them with evidence and examples, and structuring the presentation in a logical and persuasive way. It is essential to be clear about what is needed to communicate and to understand the key points that are intended to convey.

Use engaging body language: Nonverbal cues play a significant role in public speaking. Posture, gestures, and facial expressions can convey confidence, enthusiasm, and sincerity. Use open body language, maintain eye contact with the audience, and avoid distracting mannerisms like fidgeting or pacing. Appropriate body gestures and expressions should accompany the speech for maximum results.

Clear and confident speech: Speak slowly and clearly, enunciate the words, and vary the tone and pace to keep the audience engaged. Use vocal intonation to emphasize key points and inject energy and enthusiasm into the presentation. A well-modulated voice enhances authority and keeps the audience engaged. Managing anxiety or stage fright through techniques like deep breathing, positive visualization, or relaxation exercises.

Audience engagement: Start and engage the audience with a strong grabber. Personal stories, a quote from an expert or a shocking statistic-something that takes a hold of the audience and gets them hooked and open their mind to the proceeding message. Encourage participation and feedback, ask thought-provoking questions, and use humor or personal anecdotes to create a connection with the audience. Remember, the more engaged the audiences are, the more they will remember the message. Use vocal variety, body language, gestures, and eye contact to capture and maintain the audience's attention.

Storytelling: Stories have a remarkable ability to captivate audiences and evoke emotions. Incorporate personal or relevant anecdotes into the speeches to create a deeper connection with the listeners. Emotional engagement enhances authority and leaves a lasting impact. Use as much as needed and do not over do it.

Visual aids: Utilize visual aids such as slides, charts, or props to enhance the presentation. It can be used strategically to support key points, provide visual cues, and make complex information more accessible to the audience. Using visuals can be a plus point. Use it if the situation demands so. Visualization is a powerful tool that can help and build confidence and reduce anxiety.

Managing nerves and mistakes: Even seasoned speakers encounter nerves and make mistakes. Minimize nervousness by taking deep breaths and maintaining composure. When mistakes occur, acknowledge them gracefully and move forward. View mistakes as opportunities for growth rather than dwelling on them. Audiences appreciate authenticity and resilience.

Practice: Rehearse the speech to enhance fluency, timing, and overall delivery. Public speaking skills are valuable in various aspects of life, including education, career advancement, leadership roles, and community engagement. With practice and experience, individuals can improve their ability to communicate effectively and confidently in public settings. Well-prepared message requires rehearsal, with a captivating opening and a memorable conclusion.

Flexibility and adaptation: Being flexible and adjusting the delivery based on the audience's reactions, questions, or feedback is an important trait of a good public speaking. Adapting to the audience demonstrates authority and ensures effective communication. Public speaking occurs in various settings, including conferences, webinars, and podcasts. Each platform requires specific considerations, such as vocal projection for large auditoriums or utilizing visual aids for online presentations. Adapting to different platforms enhances confidence and authority in each context.

Use concrete examples: Use concrete examples to elucidate points and connect with the audience on a personal level. Using real-life examples also demonstrates that we understand the issues at hand and have experience dealing with them.

Be authentic: Be authentic when speaking publicly. This means speaking from the heart and sharing own experiences and perspectives. Authenticity builds trust and credibility with the audience, which is essential for effective communication.

Seeking diverse speaking opportunities: Challenge yourself by speaking in diverse settings and to varied audiences. Embracing different speaking opportunities broadens personal experiences, hones adaptability, and builds confidence and authority across different contexts.

Public speaking stands as a crucial skill for politicians and professionals alike. Effectively connecting with an audience and conveying a message with clarity and confidence involves several key elements. Understanding the audience, meticulous message preparation, employing engaging body language, clear and confident speech, audience engagement, and adeptly handling nerves and mistakes collectively contribute to impactful presentations.

For politicians, every uttered word carries weight and holds the potential for significant influence. Speaking with unwavering confidence and authority is imperative to effectively communicate messages and establish connections with constituents. The dynamic nature of public speaking necessitates continuous growth and refinement of this skill. Through the consistent practice of speaking with confidence and authority, speakers can not only engage but also inspire and influence their audience.

This comprehensive analysis probes into the paramount importance of confidence and authority. It explores mindset shifts, both verbal and nonverbal communication techniques, the crafting and structuring of presentations, strategies for audience engagement, and addresses the challenges and opportunities for personal growth in the realm of public speaking. The culmination of these factors contributes to the development of a speaker who can steer the niceties of public discourse with finesse, leaving a lasting impact on their audience.

To reinforce the concepts discussed, let's summarize the key takeaways:

1. Confidence and authority are crucial for successful public speaking, allowing us to connect with the audience and establish credibility.

2. Developing a strong mindset involves overcoming fear, visualizing success, and accepting the opportunity to share knowledge.

3. Verbal and nonverbal communication plays a significant role in projecting confidence and authority.

4. Developing engaging presentations requires thorough preparation, captivating openings, persuasive closures, and the utilization of visual aids.

5. Overcoming challenges and building resilience involve managing nerves and handling mistakes effectively.

6. The power of storytelling lies in its ability to connect emotionally and structure impactful messages.

7. Adapting to different speaking contexts and platforms ensures effective communication and demonstrates authority.

Public speaking is a journey, and each opportunity provides a chance to refine skills. Public speaking is a skill that can be developed with practice, preparation, and a mindset focused on confidence and authority. Words carry weight and influence, and therefore, proper choice of words and delivery is paramount for effective outcome. Speak with intent to move people to action. If nobody does anything different after listening to the speech, then the value of the speech is zero.

Importance of public speaking

The ability to communicate effectively in front of an audience is crucial for conveying ideas, inspiring action, and building credibility. Public speaking allows an individual to share knowledge, persuade others, and engage with people from diverse background. It also helps in developing self-confidence, critical thinking, and leadership abilities.

The importance of public speaking extends across personal growth and professional success, driven by key reasons:

Enhancement of communication skill: Public speaking facilitates the articulation of thoughts and ideas, enabling individuals to express themselves clearly and engage others through verbal communication. These skills find value in everyday conversations, discussions, and presentations.

Development of personal confidence: The practice of public speaking contributes to building self-confidence and self-esteem. With each experience, individuals become more adept and comfortable speaking in front of an audience, boosting their self-assurance and belief in their capabilities.

Personal and Professional advancement: Public speaking pushes individuals to develop new skills. Public speaking is highly valued in the workplace. Effective communication is integral to leadership roles, presenting ideas or proposals, conducting meetings, and addressing team.

Influence and persuasion: Mastering public speaking enhances an individual's ability to engage an audience and convey a convincing message. Whether delivering a persuasive speech, advocating for a cause, or presenting a sales pitch, this skill greatly amplifies persuasive abilities.

Networking and connections: Public speaking provides opportunities for networking and building connections. Participating in conferences, seminars, or public forums allows an individual to connect with like-minded individuals, industry professionals, and potential collaborators, expanding network and opening doors for future collaborations.

Sharing knowledge and ideas: Public speaking enables individuals to share knowledge, insights and ideas with others. By presenting information or giving speech, individuals can educate, inspire or entertain audience. The opportunity to positively impact others and contribute to the exchange of ideas is a rewarding aspect of public speaking.

Public speaking plays a critical role in personal and professional growth. It enhances communication skills, boosts confidence, facilitates career advancement, enables influence and persuasion, promotes networking, engenders personal development, and offers opportunities to share knowledge. Espousal to public speaking can lead to numerous benefits, empowering individuals to excel in various aspects of life.

CHAPTER 9

Working with the media: Handling Interviews and Press Coverage

For politicians, collaborating with the media constitutes an integral aspect of their role. Press coverage and interviews becomes pivotal, offering key moments to convey messages to the public and solidify one's reputation as a leader. The media has witnessed substantial changes in the recent years, marked by the ascent of social media platforms and the waning influence of traditional print media. This transformation has not only bestowed unprecedented direct connections between individuals, businesses, and their target audience but has also ushered in novel challenges in effectively managing and leveraging media interactions.

Media: The core of communication

Media refers to various means of communication that are used to transmit and deliver information, news, entertainment, and other forms of content to a wide audience. It encompasses different channels and platforms, such as television, radio, newspapers, magazines, websites, social media platforms, and more. Media plays a crucial role in shaping public opinion, disseminating information, and facilitating communication between individuals and communities.

When used in a singular form, the term "media" refer to a specific medium or channel of communication. Television, for instance, serves as a medium enabling the transmission of visual and audio content to a wide audience. Likewise, radio, print media, and the internet are individual mediums for conveying information.

Additionally, "media" can function as an adjective, describing something related to communication or the mass media industry. The term "media industry" encompasses businesses, organizations, and professionals involved in producing and distributing media content. Similarly, "media literacy" pertains to the ability to critically analyze and comprehend media messages, understanding the impact of media on society.

Media plays a pivotal role in shaping our society and driving communication. It serves as a powerful tool that connects people, disseminates information, and influences public opinion. From traditional platforms such as newspapers and television to the vast landscape of digital media, let us explores how media has become the heart of communication.

Media serves as a bridge that connects individuals, communities, and nations. It transcends geographical boundaries, enabling people from diverse backgrounds to exchange ideas and share experiences. Through various mediums like social media, news outlets, and online forums, individuals can engage in conversations, express their opinions, and forge connections with others who share similar interests or concerns. Media platforms provide an inclusive space where individuals can participate in discussions and contribute to the public discourse, fostering a sense of community and belonging.

Media serves as a vital information hub, delivering news and knowledge to the masses. Journalists and reporters tirelessly gather and present accurate information on a wide range of topics, from local events to global affairs. This critical function keeps the public informed and educated, enabling citizens to make informed decisions and actively participate in democratic processes. Through investigative journalism, the media holds governments, corporations, and institutions accountable, ensuring transparency and preventing the abuse of power.

Furthermore, media acts as a catalyst for social change and awareness, shedding light on pressing social issues, promoting dialogue, and amplifying the voices of marginalized communities. Documentaries, films, and investigative reports expose injustices, raise awareness, and mobilize public support for various causes. The media's power to challenge societal norms, shape public opinion, and influence policy decisions is evident. Media campaigns and advocacy initiatives leverage the reach and influence of media platforms to drive social and political change, empowering individuals to take action for a more equitable and just society.

The advent of social media platforms has revolutionized communication and transformed media dynamics. Social media allows individuals to share thoughts, experiences, and perspectives instantly with a global audience. It facilitates the rapid dissemination of information and the democratization of content creation, giving everyone the opportunity to be both creators and consumers of media. However, this rise in social media also presents challenges like misinformation, echo chambers, and the erosion of traditional journalism standards. It becomes crucial for individuals to critically evaluate information, verify sources, and engage in constructive dialogue to mitigate these challenges.

Media has seamlessly integrated into our daily lives, influencing how we perceive the world, make decisions, and interact with others. It possesses the power to shape public opinion, challenge conventional wisdom, and bring forth social change. As consumers of media, we bear the responsibility to approach information with a critical mindset, seek diverse perspectives, and engage in informed discussions.

Media functions as the core of communication in contemporary society. It serves as the connecting thread between individuals, facilitates the distribution of information, and holds the power to shape public opinion. Whether operating through conventional channels or the digital domain, media stands as a crucial force in shaping our perception of the world and propelling societal transformations.

Tips for handling interviews and press coverage

When it comes to effectively managing reputation and gaining exposure, working with the media is vital. Interviews and press coverage can significantly impact public perception and shape the narrative surrounding one's endeavors. Interviews and press coverage can be valuable opportunities to showcase expertise, message or brand.

Prepare in advance: The key to a successful interview lies in thorough preparation. Understand their style, previous work, and typical topics. Anticipate potential questions, develop talking points, and practice delivery. Preparation instills confidence, ensuring effective communication of the intended message.

Staying on message: Identify key messages for a coherent and consistent narrative throughout the interview. Keep messages concise and reflective of core values to make a lasting impact. Resist the temptation to deviate from key points or respond to provocative questions. Maintain composure, steering the conversation back to the central message for clear and consistent communication.

Building media relationship: Invest time in cultivating connections by attending events, networking, and providing valuable insights. Establishing trust and credibility increases the likelihood of positive media coverage and long-term relationships with journalists. Beyond interviews, actively contribute valuable insights or industry-related content to position oneself as a reliable resource for future media engagements.

Authenticity and genuine interaction: Be authentic and genuine during interviews. By being authentic and honest, a strong rapport and positive impression can be established. Interview is an opportunity for the interviewer to know the candidate beyond his resume. However, maintain professionalism while striking a balance between authenticity and openness. Genuine interactions create a strong rapport and leave a positive impression.

Utilize real-life examples and data: Enhance messages by incorporating real-life examples, case studies, or relevant data. This not only reinforces the message but also adds credibility to prepare some persuasive and concise examples or statistics that illustrate the impact or significance that support the message.

Stay on top of current events: Keep abreast of current news and events. This helps to provide relevant and timely insights during interviews. Being aware of the broader context allows an individual to position his message effectively and make connections to larger trends or developments.

Be mindful of non-verbal communication and voice modulation: Pay attention to body language and voice modulation. Maintain an open and engaged posture, make natural gestures, and use facial expressions to convey the message effectively. Additionally, vary voice tone, pace, and volume to emphasize important points or add emphasis. A confident and engaging presence can enhance the message and captivate the audience.

Be cautious with off-the-record comments: Exercise caution when sharing information off the record. Establish clear boundaries and agreements beforehand, understanding the rules of off-the-record conversations. Ensure clarity on what can and cannot be reported to avoid misunderstandings.

Maintain professionalism and calmness: Always be professional while dealing with the media, even when opinions differ. Treat journalists with respect. Stay calm and composed during interviews and press coverage, even if asked difficult or unexpected questions. Feel free to ask for clarification or more time to formulate responses.

Avoid Jargon and Technical Terms: Avoid using jargon and technical terms that may be confusing for the public. Instead, use plain language and simple analogies to communicate for effective result. This will ensure that the message is accessible to a wider audience and can help build reputation as a clear and effective communicator.

Be mindful of timing: Respond promptly to interview requests, showing professionalism and cooperation. Recognize journalists' tight deadlines and, if necessary, politely request a reschedule to a more suitable time, demonstrating a commitment to thorough preparation.

Follow media ethics and guidelines: Familiarize with media ethics and guidelines. Understand the importance of accuracy, objectivity, and fairness in media coverage. Avoid making unsupported claims, spreading rumors, or engaging in any unethical practices. Respecting these principles will enhance reputation and promote positive relationships with journalists.

Anticipate difficult questions: Prepare for challenging or controversial questions that may arise. Practice responding calmly and transparently while staying true to key messages. Address any concerns honestly and transparently, and it is okay to admit not knowing the answer rather than being in a controversial soup.

Be adaptable and open to feedback: Prepare for various interview formats, including live, pre-recorded, or written interviews, each with its nuances. Adapt to evolving communication styles and practice for different scenarios. Accept feedback and continuously seek to improve on the media communication skills. Actively listen to journalists' feedback or suggestions and use them to refine the approach.

Control the narrative: Take charge of the interview by steering back to the key message. If faced with questions unrelated to the message, briefly acknowledge and pivot back to prepared points. Maintain control over the narrative to ensure alignment with key messages.

Address controversial topics: When addressing controversial topics, do so sensitively and respectfully. Avoid inflammatory language or personal attacks, and focus on the issues at hand. Demonstrate leadership and a willingness to tackle difficult subjects, building a reputation as a fair and thoughtful politician.

Be aware of cultural sensitivities: If one's organization or political party operates in different regions or has a global audience, be mindful of cultural sensitivities. Understand the cultural norms and customs of the audience. Avoid making assumptions or generalizations that may offend or misrepresent certain cultures or communities.

Practice active listening: Employ active listening during interviews, paying close attention to questions and responding thoughtfully and respectfully. It also means being willing to listen to criticism or differing opinions, and responding in a constructive and respectful manner. Practicing active listening demonstrate an individual's willingness to engage with others and build credibility as a responsive and thoughtful leader.

Seek media training if needed: Consider media training if anticipating regular media engagements or facing challenges in handling interviews effectively. Media training can provide valuable skills, such as message development, interview techniques, and managing difficult situations. Enhance confidence and competence in media interactions through professional training.

Learn from each experience: Reflect on each interview, assessing strengths and areas for improvement. Assess what went well and identify those areas which may need further improvement. Consider seeking feedback from colleagues or media professionals to gain valuable insights. Learn from each experience; continue refining the skills and techniques wherever needed.

Follow up: After interviews or press coverage, express gratitude to journalists and clarify any unclear points. This follow-up contributes to building positive relationships and may lead to future coverage opportunities.

Maintain composure and refrain from becoming defensive when confronted with unfavorable press coverage. While it is natural to feel upset about perceived attacks on one's character or reputation, reacting impulsively can exacerbate the situation. Instead, adopt a calm approach and objectively assess the criticism. Reflect on its validity and take responsibility for any warranted concerns. If the criticism lacks merit, respond with facts and evidence to counter unfounded claims.

Another important aspect of working with the media is to be responsive and accessible. Journalists often work under tight deadlines, and being available to answer their questions in a timely manner can help build a positive relationship with them.

While it may be tempting to view the media as an adversary, working collaboratively with journalists can actually help us get message out to a wider audience. Building relationships with reporters and editors can also help get more favorable coverage in the future.

CHAPTER 10

Ethics and Accountability: Upholding Integrity in Politics

Ethics, a philosophical branch, delves into the principles governing right and wrong conduct, moral values, and the study of appropriate behavior in diverse situations. It involves the exploration and analysis of concepts such as fairness, justice, integrity and responsibilities. Ethics provides a framework for evaluating actions, decisions and behaviours in order to determine their moral and societal implications. It offers guidelines and standards to help individuals and communities make informed choices that are considered morally acceptable and in line with commonly accepted principles of good conduct. Ethics plays a crucial role and helps shape behavior, establish trust and promote well-being of individuals and the society as a whole.

Accountability, on the other hand, revolves around the responsibility and answerability of individuals or entities for their actions, decisions, and obligations. It encompasses the acknowledgment and acceptance of one's actions and the ensuing consequences. When held accountable, individuals are expected to explain, justify, and take responsibility for their behaviors or the outcomes of their actions.

Applicable across various contexts, including personal, professional, organizational, and governmental settings, accountability signifies that individuals or entities must act in line with specific standards, rules, or expectations. They can be called upon to provide an account of their actions to themselves, others, or a higher authority.

In organizational or institutional contexts, accountability often entails mechanisms like reporting, monitoring, and evaluation to ensure that individuals or entities fulfill their obligations and are held responsible for their performance. This approach brings forth transparency, trust, and integrity while maintaining the effectiveness and efficiency of systems and processes. In politics, upholding ethics and accountability is essential for the credibility and trustworthiness of political leaders and institutions.

Integrity, a fundamental moral and ethical principle, denotes the steadfast adherence to a set of values and principles. It encompasses traits such as honesty, trustworthiness, and consistency in one's actions, beliefs, and attitudes. Individuals with integrity are guided by a stout sense of right and wrong, showcasing ethical behavior in both their personal and professional lives.

Having integrity involves acting in harmony with one's principles, even when confronted with challenges or temptations. It requires being truthful and sincere, honoring commitments and promises, and assuming responsibility for one's actions. Those with integrity are recognized for their reliability, fairness, and accountability.

This virtue holds significant value in various life domains, including relationships, leadership roles, business transactions, and societal interactions. It serves as the bedrock for trust and respect among individuals, stimulating a sense of justice and fairness.

Maintaining integrity requires self-awareness, self-discipline, and a commitment to ethical behavior. It involves making choices and decisions that align with one's values and being transparent and accountable for one's actions. Ultimately, integrity contributes to the development of a person's character and helps build a reputation based on trust and credibility.

Integrity is a vital component of politics. Politicians are entrusted with representing the interests of their constituents and any decisions made by them will affect the lives of many people. And when a politician is not honest, his people/constituents suffers the most. Therefore, maintaining ethical standards and being accountable for their actions is not only critical for building trust and credibility with the public but for an all round progress and development.

Maintaining integrity in politics

Defining values and principles

Political leaders must take the crucial step of defining their core values and principles. These should serve as guiding lights in decision-making, ensuring actions align with stated beliefs. Integrity in politics requires adherence to ethical standards. Central to this is the principle of honesty, where politicians must be truthful in their actions, communications, and dealing with the public and their colleagues. Additionally, integrity encompasses fairness and equality, ensuring that decisions and policies are made impartially and without any favouritism.

Respect for the rule of law and democratic institutions are another crucial value. Politicians must uphold the law and respect the checks and balance of a democratic system to safeguard the rights and freedoms of citizens. Furthermore, promoting public welfare and the common good should guide political decisions, prioritizing the well-being of society over personal gains or interests.

Ultimately, a commitment to these values and principles stimulate trust between politicians and the public, strengthening democratic governance and ensuring the integrity of political processes.

Transparency and accountability

Transparency involves openness in decision-making, ensuring accessibility of information. Accountability means taking responsibility for actions and being answerable to the public. Leaders should champion transparency, openly communicating decisions, answering questions, and admitting mistakes when necessary.

Transparency and accountability are essential pillars for maintaining integrity in politics. Transparency involves openness and accessibility of information, ensuring that the actions and decisions of politicians are visible to the public. This includes disclosing financial records, disclosing conflicts of interest, and providing clear justifications for policy decisions.

Accountability on the other hand, holds politicians responsible for their actions and decisions. It involves mechanisms to ensure that politicians are answerable for their conduct, whether through elections, oversight by independent bodies, or legal recourse. Accountability nourishes trust between politicians and the public, as it demonstrates a willingness to be held to high standards of behaviour.

Together, transparency and accountability create a culture of integrity in politics, where politicians are held to account for their actions and decisions are made in the best interest of the public. This enhances public trust in government institutions and strengthens democratic governance.

Avoiding conflict of interest

Conflicts of interest can undermine the integrity of a politician. Political leaders must strive to identify, disclose, and avoid any conflicts that could compromise their decision-making abilities. This may involve disclosing financial interests, rescuing self from decisions that could benefit the self, or abstaining from voting on certain issues. When public officials prioritise personal gain over the public good, it erodes trust in the political system and undermines democracy.

Transparency is crucial; citizens have the right to know about potential conflicts so that they can hold their representatives accountable. Implementing strict regulations and enforcement mechanisms can help prevent conflicts of interest from arising in the first place.

Furthermore, promoting a culture of integrity and ethical behaviour within political institutions is essential. This can be achieved through education, training, and promoting a strong sense of duty to serve the public interest above all else.

Ultimately, by actively avoiding conflict of interest, politicians demonstrate their commitment to serving the people and upholding the principles of democracy, thereby safeguarding the integrity of the political process.

Ethical guidance and laws

Political ethics are governed by a range of guidelines and laws. Familiarize with the ethical standards and laws that apply to one's role, and follow them consistently. This may include rules around campaign finance, lobbying, and the acceptance of gifts and favors. Political leaders must adhere to and promote ethical principles, such as honesty, fairness, justice, and respect for human rights, in their actions and policies.

Ethical guidance and laws play a crucial role in maintaining integrity in politics. Clear ethical standards provide a framework for politicians to uphold honesty, transparency, and accountability in their actions. Laws serve as a deterrent against unethical behaviour and provide consequences for those who breach ethical boundaries.

Ethical guidance helps politicians navigate complex situations, ensuring they prioritise the public good over personal gain. Codes of conduct outline expectations for behaviour, including guidelines on accepting gifts, avoiding conflicts of interest and maintaining confidentiality.

Laws establish legal boundaries that governs political conduct. Campaign finance laws regulate the flow of money in politics, preventing undue influence from special interests. Anti-corruption laws prohibit bribery, extortion and other forms of illicit behaviour that undermine the integrity of political institutions.

By adhering to both ethical guidance and laws, politicians can demonstrate their commitment to serving the public trust and upholding the principles of democracy. This ensures that political decision-making remains transparent, accountable and in the best interest of the citizens.

Seeking advice and support

Integrity, defined as the adherence to moral and ethical principles, sounds simple in theory but can be difficult to uphold in practice. For those looking to preserve or restore integrity in politics, it becomes essential to seek advice and garner support from a variety of sources. Seek advice from diverse range of experts, stakeholders, colleagues and the public. This helps to prevent biases, promote informed decision-making, and ensures greater accountability.

Before diving into the strategies for maintaining integrity, it is crucial to understand why it matters. Political integrity ensures that government actions reflect the interests and values of the populace it serves, rather than serving the personal interests of the politicians. This builds trust in political institutions, fosters civic engagement, and promotes a healthier democracy.

Politicians can establish panels composed of experts in law, ethics, and public administration to provide guidance on complex issues.

Engaging in international framework that promotes good governance can provide models and support for maintaining integrity at home.

Lead by Example

In politics, where the stakes are high and the repercussions of decisions are far-reaching, the importance of leading by example cannot be overstated. Political integrity is not just a moral obligation but a foundational element that sustains the trust and confidence of the public in their leaders and the systems they govern.

One should consistently align one's actions with the principles of honesty, transparency, and accountability. When political leaders adhere to these standards, they set a powerful precedent for their peers, subordinates, and the public. This form of leadership advances a culture of integrity that can permeate through various levels of government, influencing entire political systems to improve.

Ultimately, when leaders in politics lead by example, they contribute to the development of a more ethical society. They inspire future generations of politicians and public servants to uphold the same standards, perpetuating a cycle of positive influences that can lead to more vigorous and effective governance.

By committing to lead by example, political figures can embody the change they wish to see, paving the way for a healthier democracy and a more prosperous society.

Enforcing repercussion for misconduct

Maintaining political integrity is paramount for the stability and trust in governmental institutions. However, misconduct among political figures often undermines public confidence and hampers the effective governance of a state. Enforcing strict repercussions for such misconduct is essential to uphold the law and ensure accountability.

The integrity of political offices is the cornerstone of a functioning democracy. When officials engage in misconduct, it not only tarnishes their own reputation but also casts a long shadow on the institutions they represent. The absence of stringent repercussions often leads to a cycle of impunity that can erode democratic values and lead to widespread corruption.

Political misconduct can range from corruption, embezzlement, nepotism, to abuse of power. Each of these actions can severely impact the government's ability to function transparently and efficiently. Identifying and understanding these forms of misconduct is the first step towards formulating effective deterrents.

Implementing clear, stringent laws that outline severe penalties for political misconduct is crucial. These laws must be enforced impartially and without bias to further a culture of accountability.

Enhancing transparency in governmental operations and decision-making processes helps in reducing opportunities for misconduct. Public access to information is a vital tool in monitoring and holding officials accountable.

Establishing independent ethics commissions with the power to investigate and enforce penalties is another effective strategy. These commissions should be empowered to operate without political interference.

Encouraging public participation in the political process increases scrutiny of political figures and pressures them to act ethically. Civic education on the rights and responsibilities of public officials can empower citizens to demand higher standards of integrity.

The enforcement of stringent repercussions for misconduct in maintaining political integrity is essential for sustaining public trust and ensuring the smooth functioning of democratic institutions. Through robust legislation, transparent practices, independent ethics commissions, and active public engagement, it is possible to uphold high standards of political integrity. Effective enforcement not only punishes the guilty but also serves as a deterrent for potential future misconduct, thereby strengthening the overall fabric of political governance.

Demonstrate courage and conviction

Maintaining political integrity requires not just adherence to ethical norms but also the courage and conviction to uphold these principles in the face of challenges and adversity. Political leaders and public servants must often traverse a complex terrain where interests and incentives might not always align with ethical behavior. Demonstrating courage and conviction is crucial to ensuring that integrity remains at the core of political life.

The foundation of courage and conviction in politics is a strong, principled stance. Political figures should have a clear understanding of their moral and ethical guidelines and be prepared to stand by them, even when it is unpopular or involves personal risk. This could mean resisting pressures to engage in corrupt practices or making decisions that, while difficult, are right.

Demonstrating courage involves speaking out against injustices and wrongdoing, even when the culprits are powerful individuals or institutions. This requires a commitment to transparency and justice, regardless of potential personal or political consequences. Whistle blowing, when done responsibly and legally, is a powerful tool for maintaining integrity.

Courage and conviction can be shown through transparent decision-making processes that allow public scrutiny and develop trust. This involves explaining decisions clearly, providing the rationale behind them, and showing how they align with ethical standards. This transparency ensures that the decisions are made with integrity and are free from hidden agendas.

Political environments are inherently filled with pressures from various factions and interest groups. Displaying courage means resisting these pressures when they conflict with ethical governance. It involves making decisions that are based on what is best for the public good, rather than what is best for a particular party or individual.

Ultimately, one of the most effective ways to demonstrate courage and conviction is by setting a personal example. Leaders who act with integrity inspire others in their organizations or governments to do the same. Leading by example creates a culture of integrity that can permeate an entire organization.

The path to maintaining political integrity is fraught with challenges, but it is the courage and conviction of those in power that can forge a more ethical politics. By adhering to these principles and acting with bravery and clear moral vision, political leaders can safeguard the trust placed in them by their constituents and strengthen the foundations of democratic governance. Upholding these standards is not just beneficial for individual leaders but essential for the health and stability of entire political systems.

Maintaining integrity in politics is an ongoing commitment that necessitates vigilance and leadership. By defining values and principles, practicing transparency and accountability, avoiding conflicts of interest, adhering to ethical guidelines and laws, seeking advice, leading by example, proactively addressing ethical issues, communicating effectively, acting courageously, and promoting a culture of integrity, political actors can uphold the highest standards of ethical conduct, becoming positive forces for change in the political arena.

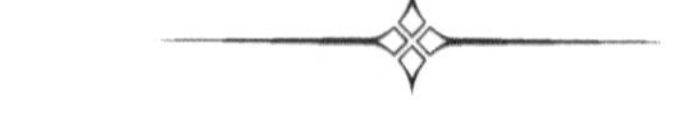

CHAPTER 11

Team Building:
Recruiting and Managing
a Strong Political Campaign

Team building is the systematic process of elevating collaboration, trust, and cooperation among a group of individuals striving towards a shared goal. This involves a spectrum of activities, exercises, and strategies geared towards enhancing communication, problem-solving, and interpersonal relationships within the team.

Team building is a crucial aspect of any organization's success. By encouraging strong relationships, effective communication, and a shared sense of purpose among team members, organizations can enhance productivity, creativity, and employee satisfaction.

The primary objectives of team building are centered on cultivating positive and cohesive team dynamics. This ensures that individuals effectively collaborate, leverage each other's strengths, and achieve optimal performance. Organizations employ team building to promote synergy, elevate morale, increase productivity, and reach greater heights collectively.

Why team matters?

Establishing a strong team is paramount for running a successful political campaign and achieving political goals. Identify skills and expertise needed-someone who can manage social media accounts, write speeches or coordinate events and so forth. However the process of team building should be slow but strong. But, why is a team so important?

Enhanced communication

Effective team building activities provides opportunities for individuals to interact, communicate, and collaborate with one another outside of their daily work routines. These interactions break down barriers, encourage open dialogue, and encourage a culture of trust and respect.

Building trust

Trust is the linchpin of a strong team. Team building activities help to establish trust among team members, leading to increased collaboration and support. A team built on trust and common goals will deliver better result than a team built on the premise of professionalism alone.

Improved collaboration

Team building exercises facilitate the development of collaborative skills, enabling team members to leverage each other's strengths and work towards common goals. Collaborative environments encourage the sharing of diverse perspectives, sharing of ideas, and contribute their unique skills leading to innovative solutions and better decision-making.

Increased productivity

A cohesive team is a productive team. When individuals feel connected and valued, they are more motivated to contribute their best efforts. Team building activities help to align team members' goals, clarify roles and responsibilities, and promote a supportive work environment, all of which contribute to improved productivity.

Encouraging creativity and innovation

By promoting open communication and cultivating a positive team culture, team building activities spark creativity and innovative thinking within the group. This culture encourages members to comfortably share their ideas, thoughts, and perspectives. This exchange of ideas often leads to unexpected connections and ignites innovative solutions. When team members feel empowered to share their insights regardless of job titles or seniority, it creates an inclusive environment that values creativity and diverse perspectives. This inclusivity can result in breakthrough innovations, as ideas emerge from various sources and levels within the team.

Strengthened problem-solving skills

Team building exercises often involve solving complex challenges, encouraging team members to think critically, analyze situations from different angles, and find creative solutions together. These experiences cultivate problem-solving skills that can be applied to real-world work scenarios. The diverse backgrounds, skills and experiences of the team members bring variety of perspectives to problem solving discussions, promoting creative thinking and considering alternative solutions.

Boosting morale and motivation

Engaging team members in fun and challenging activities can improve morale, motivation, and job satisfaction, leading to increased productivity and performance. A positive team culture established through team building activities creates a sense of belonging and camaraderie among team members. When employees feel valued and supported, they are more likely to be satisfied with their work, leading to increased job satisfaction and reduced turnover rates.

Overall, team building plays a crucial role in developing a cohesive and high-performing team by strengthening interpersonal relationships, promoting effective communication, and nurturing a positive team culture.

Practical Strategies for Effective Team Building

Clear goal setting

Establish a clear purpose, objectives, and expected outcomes for the team. After assembling the team, effectively manage them to ensure everyone is aligned toward a common goal, providing direction and motivation. Regularly offer feedback and support, and delegate responsibilities as necessary. Cultivate a positive and collaborative team environment where each member feels valued and motivated to contribute to shared objectives.

Communication and active listening

Encourage open communication by establishing channels for feedback, regular team meetings, and one-on-one discussions. Actively listen to team members' ideas, concerns, and suggestions to further an inclusive and collaborative environment. Open communication is essential as it provides ideas to pour in freely from diverse experiences of members in the team. We get to have unrestrained choices in the midst of ideas and innovations.

Icebreaker activities

Start team meetings or workshops with icebreaker activities to create a relaxed and comfortable atmosphere. Icebreakers can include sharing personal stories, playing games, or engaging in team-building exercises. This is the most common way to make the members feel at ease.

Team-building workshops and retreats

Organize workshop, seminars or group discussions focused on team building for continuous learning and development. These events provide an opportunity for team members to bond, develop trust, and engage in activities designed to enhance teamwork, problem-solving, and communication skills. Provide opportunities for professional development and growth. Encourage the team members to attend training programs, conferences, and other events where they can learn new skills and network with other political professionals. This can benefit the team members to bring new ideas and perspectives back to the team.

Recognition and appreciation

Acknowledge and celebrate team members' accomplishments. Recognize individual contributions and milestones achieved collectively, develop a culture of appreciation and motivation. Show appreciation for their hard work and dedication, and recognize their achievements publicly. It is innate for individual to seek little attention when working for a greater cause beyond the self.

Effective team building transcends mere organization of enjoyable activities; it involves creating an environment where individual feels valued, connected, and empowered to collaborate towards shared goals. Through investment in team-building strategies, organizations can encourage collaboration, elevate productivity, and ultimately attain greater success. Building a tough team is an ongoing process that demands commitment, communication, and a shared vision for success.

Recruitment and management

Successfully managing a political campaign necessitates a well-coordinated team and effective management strategies. The recruitment and management of campaign staff plays pivotal roles in determining the success or failure of a political endeavor. From identifying key positions to implementing efficient management techniques, we will delve into the essential steps and strategies needed to construct a winning campaign team.

Defining key positions

Campaign Manager/ Chief Agent

The campaign manager is the central figure responsible for overseeing all aspects of the campaign. The role of a campaign manager in an election is vital in orchestrating and executing successful political campaigns. The campaign manager serves as the primary strategist and coordinator, responsible for various aspects of the campaign.

> *Strategic planning:* The campaign manager identifies the campaign's goals, develops a strategic plan, and outlines the overall campaign strategy. This includes setting target demographics, determining messaging strategies, and devising a campaign timeline.

> *Team management:* The campaign manager recruits, assembles, and manages a team of staff and volunteers responsible for executing different campaign activities. This involves assigning tasks, providing guidance and leadership, and developing a positive working environment.

> *Fundraising:* A campaign manager plays a vital role in fundraising efforts by devising a fundraising plan, identifying potential donors, organizing campaign events

and coordinating fundraising drives. They work closely with finance teams to ensure the campaign's financial stability.

➤ *Message development:* Developing and refining the campaign's message is a critical responsibility. The campaign manager collaborates with communication experts to create a persuasive narrative and consistent messaging that resonates with voters.

➤ *Voter outreach:* The campaign manager oversees various voter outreach initiatives, including devising a voter contact strategy, mobilizing volunteers for door-to-door canvassing, organizing phone banks and coordinating public events like rallies and town halls.

➤ *Data analysis and targeting:* A campaign manager works with data analysts to utilize voter data for targeting and prioritizing campaign efforts. This involves identifying key demographics, tracking voter trends and making data-driven decisions.

➤ *Media relations:* Managing media interactions and building relationships with journalists and news outlets is crucial. The campaign manager coordinates press releases, press conferences, and interviews to ensure effective media coverage and messaging.

➤ *Ground operations:* The campaign manager oversees the day-to-day logistics of the campaign, including field operations, event planning, and volunteers' coordination and managing campaign offices.

➤ *Crisis management:* In times of crisis or unexpected events, the campaign manager plays a pivotal role in managing and containing potential damage. They must think quickly, adapt strategies, and effectively communicate to mitigate any negative impact on the campaign.

> *Compliance and reporting*: A campaign manager ensures campaign activities adhere to legal and ethical guidelines. This includes compliance with campaign finance laws, filing required reports, and maintaining transparency.

The role of a campaign manager requires strong leadership, strategic thinking, excellent communication skills, and the ability to coordinate multiple campaign components. Their efforts are instrumental in shaping the campaign's messaging, mobilizing volunteers, engaging with voters, and ultimately maximizing the chances of electoral success.

Communications Director

The communications director holds the crucial responsibility of shaping and conveying the campaign's message to the public. Possessing excellent written and verbal communication skills, as well as expertise in media relations and social media management, is essential for this role.

> *Strategic communication planning:* The communication director plays a key role in developing the overall communication strategy for the election campaign. This involves setting clear objectives, identifying target audiences, and developing messages that align with the candidate's vision and goals.

> *Message development:* The communication director works closely with the candidate and campaign team to develop messages that resonates with voters. They ensure that the messages are consistent, authentic, and effectively communicate the candidate's values, policies and vision for the future.

> *Media relations:* The communication director acts as the primary point of contact for the media. They build relationships with the journalists, pitch stories and coordinate interviews and press conference. They are responsible for managing the campaign's media coverage, ensuring accurate and fovourable portrayal of the candidate.

> *Digital communication:* The communication director must have a strong online presence strategy. This includes managing social media platforms, website content, and online advertising campaigns. They leverage digital tools to reach a wider audience, engage with supporters, and counter misinformation.

> *Crisis management:* Elections can be challenging and unexpected situations may arise. The communication director must be prepared to handle crises effectively, quickly responding to negative events or media narratives that could impact the campaign. They develop crisis communication plans, coordinate messaging, and provide guidance to the candidate and campaign team during turbulent times.

> *Collaboration and coordination:* The communication director works closely with the campaign staff, including the campaign manager, policy advisors, and fundraising team to ensure alignment across all communication efforts. They provide guidance and training to campaign spokespeople and coordinate messaging consistently across various platforms.

Field Director

Field directors typically work for political campaigns, parties, or advocacy organizations and are responsible for overseeing the grassroots operations, volunteer management and voter outreach efforts. This position requires someone with strong interpersonal skills, the ability to mobilize supporters, and a keen understanding of the local political dominion.

> *Campaign strategy:* Field directors collaborate with the campaign managers and strategists to develop an effective ground game strategy. They analyse voter data, demographics, and polling information to determine target precincts and devise a plan to engage and mobilise voters.

> *Field organizing:* Field directors are in charge of recruiting, training and supervising a team of field organisers and volunteers. They organize door-to-door canvassing, phone- banking, voter registration drives and other grassroots activities to create a strong campaign presence within the community.

> *Voter contact:* They ensure the campaign's messaging is delivered effectively to voters through direct voter contact methods like canvassing, phone calls, and text messaging. They might also coordinate town hall and community meetings, rallies and other events to engage with voters directly.

> *Data collection and analysis:* Field directors oversee the collection of data through various field operations. They ensure that accurate information is generated during canvassing or phone banking, which helps in creating targeted voter databases and analyzing voter preferences. This information shapes campaign strategies and assists in resource allocation.

> *Field operations management:* Field directors coordinate logistical aspects of field operations. They plan and manage the campaign's field budget, oversees the distribution of campaign materials (such as yard signs

and campaign literature), and track and report progress to the campaign manager.

➢ *Collaboration and communication:* Field directors serve as a bridge between the field team, campaign leadership, and other stakeholders. They ensure effective communication and coordination between different campaign departments, volunteers, and community organizations. They may also work loosely with media and public relations team to amplify the campaign's reach.

➢ *Training and development:* Field directors provide training and guidance to field organisers and volunteers, ensuring they have the necessary skills to effectively engage with voters. They may conduct workshops on canvassing techniques, phone-banking strategies, voter registration procedures, and data collection methods. This helps maintain a well-trained field team capable of executing the campaign's goals.

➢ *Targeting and voter identification:* Field directors work with their team to identify and prioritize key voter segments and demographics. They analyse voter registration data, conduct surveys, and utilize voter modeling tools to identify potential supporters and undecided voters. This information helps tailor outreach efforts and messaging to specific audiences.

➢ *Community outreach:* Field directors build relationships with local community leaders, organizations and influencers to build a strong network of support. They coordinate with these stakeholders to organise community events, forums, or neighbourhood meetings where the campaign can connect with residents, address concerns, and listen to local issues.

> *Field reporting and evaluation:* Field directors are responsible for tracking and reporting the progress of grassroots efforts. They monitor and analyse field data, including the number of voter contacts, canvassing outcomes, and volunteer engagement statistics. These insights allow them to evaluate the effectiveness of different strategies and make adjustments to improve overall campaign performance.

> *Crisis and rapid response:* Field directors must be ready to respond swiftly to unforeseen events or crisis during the campaign. They should have contingency plans in place and work closely with the communication team to address issues, manage messaging, and mobilise resources if necessary.

> *GOTV (Get out the vote) efforts:* As Election day nears; field directors play crucial roles in organizing robust GOTV initiatives. They develop strategies to mobilise supporters, promote early voting options, arrange transportation to polling stations, and ensure that supporters cast their votes. This final push aims to maximize voter turnout and boost the campaign's chances of success.

Field directors are pivotal in executing the ground game strategies for an election campaign. Through effective leadership, organization and engagement strategies, they drive a campaign's grassroots efforts, ensuring that the candidate's message reaches and resonates with voters, ultimately contributing to the campaign's overall success.

Finance Director

The role of a finance director in an election is primarily focused on managing the financial aspects of a campaign. They play a crucial role in ensuring that the campaign's financial resources are effectively utilized and reported in accordance with the legal and ethical guidelines. Some key responsibilities of a finance director in an election may include:

> *Fundraising:* The finance director is responsible for devising and implementing strategies to raise funds for the campaign. This can involve organizing fundraising events, coordinating with donors, and managing online fundraising platforms.

> *Budgeting:* They develop and oversee the campaign budget, allocating resources to various activities such as advertising, staff salaries, travel expenses and voter outreach. Monitoring and controlling campaign expenditures are a critical responsibility.

> *Compliance and reporting:* The finance director ensures that campaign finance laws and regulations are allowed. They maintain proper financial records, track contributions and timely file reports with the appropriate authorities.

> *Financial strategy and adjustments:* Working closely with the campaign manager and other key stakeholders, the finance director helps develop financial strategies to support the campaign's goals and objectives. The finance director continuously monitors the financial aspects and adjusts the campaign's financial strategy as needed. This can involve reallocating resources, revising fundraising targets, or adapting spending plans based on changing circumstances, such as shifts in public opinion or competitor activities.

> *Risk management:* They assess financial risks and implement measures to mitigate them. This includes monitoring and addressing any potential issues related

to campaign finance, such as improper donations or misappropriation of funds.

> *Communication:* The finance director communicates with donors, supporters and other stakeholders to provide financial updates, acknowledge contributions, and maintain transparency. They may also collaborate with the communication team to draft messaging around campaign finances.

> *Compliance and ethics:* The finance director is responsible for educating campaign staff and volunteers about campaign finance regulations and ethical practices. They implement internal control measures to ensure that the campaign stays within legal boundaries and avoids any improprieties. They are responsible for providing accurate and timely financial statements, maintaining records that are accessible to the public and complying with any transparency requirements set by regulatory bodies.

> *Financial analysis:* The finance director conducts financial analysis to assess the campaign's financial health and performances. This includes monitoring fundraising trends, analyzing expenditure patterns and providing insights to inform strategic decision-making.

> *Donor relationships management:* Developing and maintaining relationships with donors is a crucial aspect of the finance director's role. They work to cultivate long-term relationships with individuals, organizations, and establishments that support the campaign financially, ensuring donor satisfaction and potentially securing future contributions.

> *Audit and legal support:* The finance director collaborates with auditors and legal advisors to facilitate audits and

address any legal matters related to campaign finance. They ensure that all financial records are prepared and presented in a manner that withstands scrutiny and satisfies legal requirements.

Overall, the finance director is a critical figure in an election campaign, entrusted with the responsibility of managing and maximizing the financial resources available to support the campaign's goals. Their expertise in fundraising, budgeting, compliance and financial strategy helps ensure the campaign operates smoothly, maintains financial integrity and sustains its financial viability throughout the election period.

Developing a comprehensive Recruitment Strategies

Clearly define roles and responsibilities: Before recruiting campaign staff, develop detailed job descriptions outlining the roles and responsibilities of each position. Clearly define expectations, qualifications, and desired skills for potential candidates.

Network and tap into existing resources: Leverage personal and professional networks to identify individuals who might be interested in joining the campaign. Reach out to political organizations, local party affiliates, and volunteers from previous campaigns who have demonstrated commitment and competence.

Advertise open positions: Utilize online platforms, social media, and local community networks to advertise open campaign positions. Consider posting job listings on political websites, local newspapers, and social media groups to reach a wider audience.

Conduct thorough interviews: When interviewing candidates, ask relevant questions to assess their skills, experience, and commitment. Look for individuals who align with the campaign's values, demonstrate enthusiasm, and possess the necessary expertise for their respective roles.

Evaluate cultural fit: Building a cohesive campaign team requires individuals who can work well together. Consider the team dynamics and how potential candidates may fit into the existing culture. Encourage open and honest communication during the interview process.

Building and managing the team

Establish clear communication channels: Implement effective communication channels to ensure efficient information flow within the team. Regular meetings, email updates, and communication tools like project management software can facilitate coordination and collaboration.

Stimulate a positive work environment: Create a supportive and inclusive work environment where team members feel valued and motivated. Encourage open dialogue, provide constructive feedback, and recognize individual and team achievements.

Set realistic goals and expectations: Develop clear campaign goals and targets that align with the overall campaign strategy. Ensure that each team member understands their individual goals and the collective objectives. Regularly monitor progress and provide necessary guidance and support.

Delegate tasks appropriately: Assign tasks and responsibilities based on individuals' strengths and expertise. Delegating effectively allows team members to focus on areas where they can contribute most effectively, creating a sense of ownership and empowerment.

Invest in training and skill development: Offer training opportunities to enhance the skills and knowledge of campaign staff. This could include workshops, seminars, or online courses. Empowering team members with additional skills can improve their performance and contribute to long-term success.

Encourage collaboration and teamwork: Promote collaboration among team members by organizing brainstorming sessions, team-building exercises, and collaborative projects. Encourage cross-departmental collaboration to leverage diverse perspectives and strengthen the campaign's strategy.

Manage conflict effectively: Address conflicts and disagreements within the team promptly and constructively. Encourage open communication, active listening, and mediation techniques to resolve issues and maintain team cohesion.

Recruiting and managing a strong political campaign requires careful planning, strategic thinking, and effective leadership. By identifying key positions, implementing robust recruitment strategies, and stimulating a positive and collaborative work environment, political campaigns can assemble a dedicated and high-performing team. Successful campaign management involves clear communication, goal setting, appropriate delegation, and continuous skill development. Remember, a strong campaign team can make all the difference in achieving electoral success and making a lasting impact on the political setting.

Building Coalitions and Alliances

Building coalitions and alliances is an essential component of any successful political campaign. Identify organizations and leaders that share similar values and priorities such as community groups, labor unions, business organizations, and advocacy groups. Initiate contact with these entities, sharing the campaign's vision and goals. By working with other organizations and leaders of the community, messages can be easily amplified for broader audience.

Forge strong relationships with these organizations and leaders, emphasizing trust and mutual respect. Invest time and resources in cultivating these connections, attending community events, participating in meetings, and engaging in joint projects. In addition to building relationships with other organizations and leaders, it is important to be strategic in engaging with them. Identify specific areas of common interest and collaborate to advance shared goals. This may involve joint efforts on voter registration drives, community service projects, or policy advocacy campaigns.

Building coalitions and alliances helps to expand influence, and create the chance to increase the impact of the campaign. It also builds a network of support groups that can help to overcome obstacles and challenges throughout the campaign. In electoral politics, effective team building serves as a fundamental principle to access power through voter support, ultimately achieving political goals. The better the team is managed, the higher the chances of success. Therefore, practical strategies for team building, task classification, and team management become essential for a successful political campaign.

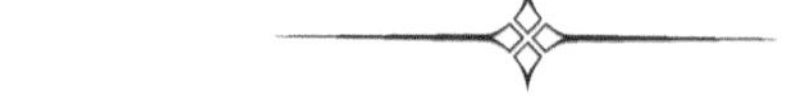

CHAPTER 12

Negotiation:
Collaboration and Camaraderie

Negotiation is the process of discussing and reaching an agreement or settlement between two or more parties who have differing interests, goals, or positions. It involves engaging in dialogue, making compromises, and finding common ground to resolve conflicts or achieve mutually beneficial outcomes. It is a complex and dynamic process that plays a vital role in various aspects of lives, ranging from personal relationships to business transactions. It is an art that requires effective communication, strategic thinking and a deep understanding of human psychology.

In a negotiation, the parties involved may have competing interests or viewpoints, and the goal is to reach a compromise or agreement that satisfies the needs and concerns of all parties to the greatest extent possible. Negotiation can occur in various contexts, including politics, business, diplomacy, and personal relationships.

The process of negotiation typically involves:

Communication: Effective negotiation hinges on adept communication, encompassing both verbal and non-verbal cues.

The ability to articulate interests and comprehend the concerns of the other party is paramount for success in any negotiations.

Strategic Bargaining: Understanding the relative strengths and weaknesses of both parties can help in determining the appropriate strategies to leverage those factors effectively. Leveraging factors such as alternative options or additional resources can significantly influence negotiation dynamics, enhancing one's position. Making proposals, counterproposals, and judicious concessions promote middle-ground exploration, paving the way for mutually beneficial agreements.

Problem-solving prowess: Aiming for mutual benefit and sustainable agreements necessitates a win-win mentality. Exploring creative solutions, brainstorming and engaging in problem-solving can help bridge gaps and generate innovative outcomes.

Relationships building: Establishing trust, nurturing rapport, and cultivating positive working relationships with all parties involved enriches the negotiation process. These relationships are integral to a collaborative atmosphere, enhancing the likelihood of reaching agreements that stand the test of time.

Negotiation is a dynamic and fluid process, demanding active listening, effective communication, strategic thinking, and the ability to analyze and evaluate diverse options. Embracing the give-and-take nature of negotiations, while considering both short-term and long-term implications, is fundamental to achieving successful outcomes.

Successful negotiation skills are essential for politicians as they collaborate with other politicians, stakeholders, and communities to advance their goals and work towards positive outcomes. Through negotiation, politicians can map read differences, find common ground, and reach agreements that serve the best interests of their constituents and the broader community.

There are certain premises worth considering before venturing into the complexities of negotiation and aftermath. A successful negotiation largely depends on many factors which are interwoven and interconnected. And such understanding would provide for a more matured and sustained results.

Let us consider the following nature and features of negotiation:

Understanding the dynamics of negotiation: Negotiation stands as a dynamic process wherein two or more parties collaborate to discover common ground. Active participation, effective communication, and a readiness to compromise are integral to this process. Typically, negotiation unfolds through key stages, including preparation, discussion, proposal, bargaining, and agreement. Each stage holds a pivotal role in achieving successful outcomes.

Importance of negotiation in politics: Negotiation is the backbone of politics, enabling politicians to steer complex issues, find common ground and making informed decisions. It acts as a bridge, connecting different ideologies, bringing consensus, and shaping policies for the greater good. Politicians with effective negotiation skills can build trust, nurture relationships, and successfully realize their goals.

Effective strategies for negotiation with politicians: When engaging in negotiations with politicians, adopting a collaborative mindset is crucial. Building rapport and establishing a foundation of trust become pivotal elements for success. Employing active listening, empathy, and a nuanced understanding of the political setting enhances communication effectiveness. Additionally, thorough preparation, a clear agenda, and presenting persuasive arguments significantly influence the negotiation process.

Collaboration with stakeholders: In the negotiation process, involving stakeholders is imperative for consensus-building and ensuring the consideration of all parties' interests. Effective collaboration with stakeholders necessitates open communication, transparency, and a willingness to address their concerns. Politicians, by actively engaging stakeholders in the negotiation process, can formulate policies that are not only inclusive but also sustainable in the long run.

Key tenets of successful negotiation: Firstly, it requires a win-win mindset, where all parties involved feel satisfied with the outcome. Secondly, effective negotiation involves the ability to identify and prioritise common interests. Thirdly, flexibility and adaptability are crucial for finding creative solutions and overcoming obstacles. Lastly, maintaining open lines of communication and trust are essential for building long-term relationships.

Elevating negotiation skills: Negotiation is a skill that can be honed and improved over time. By investing in personal development and training, politicians and stakeholders can enhance their negotiation skills. Learning effective communication techniques, conflict resolution strategies and understanding cultural differences can significantly impact the negotiation process. Continuous learning and practical application are indispensable for evolving into adept negotiators.

Conquering challenges in negotiation: Negotiations, particularly in the politics, present formidable challenges. Conflicting interests, power dynamics and differing ideologies can create obstacles. However, a collaborative approach, active listening, and the pursuit of common ground can surmount these challenges.

Constructing relationships founded on trust and respect becomes paramount for navigating difficult negotiations successfully.

Negotiation stands as a pivotal skill for politicians engaged in collaborative efforts with peers and stakeholders. It encompasses the art of discovering common ground, resolving conflicts, building robust relationships, and ultimately achieving mutually beneficial agreements. This skill proves indispensable for politicians working towards policy goals, whether navigating bipartisan bills or securing funding for local projects. Successful negotiation demands a delicate blend of strategy and empathy.

The Power of Collaboration

Imagine this: You're stranded on a deserted island (metaphorically speaking, of course). You could either attempt to survive solo, Robinson Crusoe-style, or you could team up with your fellow castaways and work together to build a raft, hunt for food, and ultimately escape the island. Spoiler alert: Collaboration is the key to survival—and success.

Collaboration is more than just a buzzword; it's a fundamental principle that drives innovation and progress. By pooling resources, sharing knowledge, and combining strengths, individuals and organizations can achieve far more than they ever could alone. So, the next time you're faced with a daunting challenge, don't hesitate to reach out and collaborate with others. After all, teamwork makes the dream work.

Effective strategies for collaborative negotiation

Preparation: Prepare thoroughly before entering into a negotiation. This involves comprehensive research on the issue at hand, a deep understanding of the interests and positions of other parties, and clear identification of one's goals and priorities.

Gather any relevant data or information that can support one's arguments during the negotiation.

Understand the interests and motivations: Prior to negotiations, invest time in understanding the interests and motivations of all involved parties. What are their priorities and goals? What do they hope to achieve from the negotiation? By understanding their perspective, a better frame of arguments and directions can be made and finding areas of potential agreement can be done easier. Understanding underlying interests and motivations leads to more effective and collaborative solutions.

Active listening and communication: Effective negotiation requires active listening and clear communication. It is crucial to genuinely hear and comprehend the perspectives and concerns of other parties. Actively listen, ask clarifying questions and ensure that the points are communicated clearly and respectfully. Utilize open-ended questions and seek clarification to have a clear understanding of their position.

Generate options and establish common ground: Collaboratively generate a range of options that address the interest and concerns of all parties involved. Brainstorming and exploring alternative solutions can help find creative and mutually beneficial outcomes. Stimulate an open and inclusive environment where stakeholders feel comfortable expressing their ideas and contributing to the process. Look for shared interests and values that can serve as a basis for cooperation. Emphasize the mutual benefits of reaching an agreement.

Negotiate and make concession: Negotiation is a nuanced process demanding flexibility and a readiness to compromise. After generating options, delve into the negotiation phase. Demonstrate a willingness to make concessions and seek compromises where applicable. Given that negotiation often involves give-and-take, prioritize goals and evaluate potential trade-offs. Effectiveness in this step relies on articulate communication, persuasive arguments, and a commitment to finding common ground. Remember, negotiation aims at a mutually beneficial solution rather than a win or loss. Establish an environment where all parties express their views openly and respectfully. Actively listen, show empathy, and refrain from personal attacks or adversarial behavior, as these can impede productive negotiations.

Establishing trust: Honesty and transparency in communication, coupled with commitment follow-through, lays the foundation for building positive relationships. Honesty helps create a favorable relationship with the other party, simplifying future negotiations. Essential for successful negotiation is the cultivation of positive relationships with fellow politicians and stakeholders. Invest time in getting to know them, attentively listen to their concerns, and develop trust. Building rapport and maintaining open communication lines contribute to a more collaborative and productive negotiation environment.

Maintaining composure: Negotiations can be stressful, but maintaining a calm and professional demeanor is crucial. Avoid letting emotions take control or personalizing matters. Instead, concentrate on the pertinent issues and strive to find solutions that benefit everyone involved.

Seek win-win solutions: In negotiation, the pursuit of win-win solutions stands paramount. This requires creativity and collaboration, leading to more sustainable and effective outcomes. Be open to exploring creative solutions that address the concerns of all parties involved. Think outside the box and consider innovative approaches that may not have been previously considered. Sometimes, a win-win outcome can be achieved by finding alternative options that satisfy the underlying interests of all stakeholders.

Seal the agreement: The pinnacle of negotiation is achieving an agreement that harmonizes with the interests of all involved parties. It involves finding compromises and making concessions. Ensure that the final agreement is fair and square benefiting all the parties involved. Rigorously scrutinize the terms and ensure that they are clear, actionable, and acceptable to all the parties.

Maintain a long-term perspective: Remember that negotiations in politics are often part of a larger context. Deliberate on the long-term implications of the agreements and how they align with overarching goals and values. Aspire towards outcomes that not only fulfill immediate needs but also contribute to the overarching vision for the community or constituency represented.

Implementation and follow-up: Post-agreement, shift focus towards diligent implementation. Establish a clear timeline, allocate responsibilities, and devise a monitoring mechanism for progress. Regular communication and follow-ups with stakeholders ensure effective implementation and provide a platform to address any emerging issues or concerns.

Negotiation, with its inherent complexities, demands patience, flexibility, and a collaborative spirit. Adhering to these guidelines enhances the likelihood of achieving successful outcomes when collaborating with fellow politicians and stakeholders.

The art of negotiation stands as a pivotal skill for politicians. Through the establishment of common ground, active listening, flexibility, trust-building, maintaining composure, pursuing win-win solutions, and thorough preparation, politicians can effectively collaborate with peers and stakeholders to realize their policy goals. Employing these strategic approaches enables politicians to engage in effective negotiations, cultivate robust relationships, and promote collaboration with fellow politicians and stakeholders. Possessing successful negotiation skills proves indispensable in achieving mutually beneficial outcomes and advancing the interests of the constituents and communities they serve.

CHAPTER 13

Conflict Resolution:
Managing Disagreements and Challenges

Conflict is an inevitable facet of life, impacting both personal and professional spheres. However, the way we handle conflicts plays a pivotal role in maintaining healthy relationships and achieving goals. This leads us to the fundamental question:

What is conflict?

Conflict refers to a state of disagreement, opposition, or discord between individuals, groups, organizations, or even nations. It emerges when there's a clash of interests, values, needs, or goals. Conflict can manifest in various contexts, such as personal relationships, workplaces, social settings, or international affairs.

In its diverse forms, conflict includes verbal disputes, misunderstandings, power struggles, ideological differences, or even physical confrontations. These may stem from competing interests, resource scarcity, divergent perspectives, or unresolved issues.

Conflicts yield both positive and negative outcomes. Healthy conflicts involve open and respectful communication, enabling parties to express differences constructively and engage in dialogue for resolution. Conversely, unhealthy conflicts encompass destructive communication, personal attacks, or a reluctance to find common ground. Conflict, on one hand, can lead to growth, change, and the exploration of new ideas, innovation, creativity, and deeper understanding. On the other hand, conflicts may result in negative consequences such as damaged relationships, reduced productivity, emotional stress, or even violence.

A multitude of factors can fuel conflicts, often exacerbated by emotions like anger, fear, or resentment, complicating the resolution process. Conflicts span various scales, from minor disagreements between individuals to large-scale conflicts involving communities or nations. In personal relationships, conflicts may arise from communication breakdowns, trust issues, jealousy, or diverging expectations. In the workplace, conflicts might stem from power struggles, competition for resources, conflicting priorities, or interpersonal tensions among colleagues or managers.

When left unaddressed, conflicts can yield detrimental effects, escalating, intensifying, and becoming more challenging to resolve. This progression can lead to entrenched animosity and disrupted relationships, and in extreme cases, conflicts may escalate to legal disputes, physical violence, or even wars.

Mastering effective conflict management is a crucial skill in interpersonal, professional, and societal settings. It encompasses communication, negotiation, compromise, active listening, empathy, and the pursuit of mutually beneficial solutions. The goal of conflict resolution is to transform conflicts into opportunities for constructive dialogue and peaceful resolution, minimizing harm and restoring peace.

Conflict resolution involves addressing and resolving disagreements, disputes, or conflicts between two or more parties.

It seeks a peaceful and mutually acceptable solution, minimizing negative consequences and bringing understanding and cooperation. This process employs various strategies, techniques, and communication skills aimed at addressing underlying causes, facilitating dialogue, and creating a collaborative environment for problem-solving.

The ultimate objective of conflict resolution is to reach a resolution that is fair, equitable, and acceptable that satisfies the needs and concerns of all parties involved, while maintaining or improving relationships and preventing further escalation of the conflict. It is an essential skill in personal, professional and social contexts, contributing to effective teamwork, negotiation, mediation, and overall social harmony.

Notably, conflict resolution doesn't seek to declare winners or losers. Instead, its focus is on reaching a compromise or agreement that satisfies the needs and interests of all parties to the greatest extent possible.

Key aspects of conflict resolution

Voluntary participation: Engagement in conflict resolution processes is typically a voluntary choice. The involved parties willingly opt for dialogue and seek resolution rather than resorting to force or coercion. This voluntary nature helps create an environment conducive to open communication and collaboration.

Voluntary compliance: Resolutions achieved through conflict resolution are typically based on voluntary compliance. Parties agree to abide by the terms and commitments outlined in the resolution, ensuring that the resolution is sustainable and implemented in good faith.

Non-violent: Conflict resolution seeks to resolve conflicts without resorting to violence, intimidation, or aggression. It emphasizes peaceful means and constructive dialogue to address disputes. Non-violence is a fundamental principle underlying conflict resolution efforts, promoting respect for human rights and the dignity of all parties involved.

Fair and equitable: Conflict resolution aims to achieve fair and equitable outcomes that consider the needs and interests of all the parties involved. It works to address power imbalances and promote justice in resolving conflicts, with fairness and equity serving as essential principles for long-lasting and sustainable resolutions.

Communication and active listening: Effective communication and active listening are at the core of conflict resolution. This involves creating a safe and respectful environment where all parties can express their perspectives, concerns, and interests. Active listening helps to establish empathy, understanding, and the ability to identify underlying needs and motivations.

Continuous process: Recognizing conflict resolution as a continuous and ongoing process acknowledges that conflicts may evolve, new issues may arise, and resolutions may require adjustments or reassessment over time. Conflict resolution efforts can include mechanisms for ongoing dialogue, monitoring, and evaluation to ensure the effectiveness and adaptability of the resolution.

By understanding the nature and characteristics of conflict resolution, individuals and organizations can approach conflicts with a constructive and collaborative mindset. Through voluntary participation, cooperative problem-solving, fairness, effective communication, and a commitment to non-violence, conflict resolution processes can contribute to sustainable and peaceful resolutions.

Conflict management

Effectively handling disagreement and challenges in conflicts necessitates adept communication, understanding, and a collaborative approach. Conflict resolution is crucial for maintaining harmonious relationships, enhancing team work and promoting productivity. It allows individual to express their concerns, find common ground and reach mutually beneficial solutions. By promptly and constructively addressing conflicts, individuals can prevent their escalation into more significant issues that might damage relationships and impede progress.

For a politician, conflicts and challenges are inevitable. Whether dealing a disagreement with a fellow politician or facing challenges from the constituents, conflict resolution skills are essential to finding a solution and moving forward.

Some conflicts and challenges may not readily yield to direct negotiation or collaboration. In such cases, strong leadership skills can guide the team or constituents through the situation.

Tips to address and resolve conflicts

Stay calm and listen: Maintain composure when disagreements arise. Approach the situation with professionalism, avoiding being swayed by emotions. Focus, take a deep breath, and tackle the situation with a level head. While the situation may demand quick and decisive action, remaining calm under pressure is crucial. Base decisions on the best available information. Actively listen to the other person's perspective without interruption or defensiveness. Create a safe space for both parties to express their thoughts and feelings.

Seek common ground: Identify areas of agreement or shared goals between both parties. Finding common ground can lay the foundation for resolving conflicts. Even in the midst of disagreement, there is often some shared ground that can be discovered. Look for common goals or interests as a basis for a solution.

Choose the right time and place: Create conducive environment for open and honest dialogue, ensuring privacy and minimizing distractions. Recognize when to intervene and when not to, as conflicts are often complex and delicate situations.

Empathize and understand: Make an effort to understand the other person's perspective. Put yourself in their shoes and acknowledge their emotions and concerns. Respecting each participant's viewpoint and demonstrating empathy towards their feelings and concerns allows an environment of trust and mutual understanding. Empathy enables individuals to recognize and validate others' emotions, facilitating a more constructive resolution process.

Communicate openly and respectfully: Express thoughts clearly, confidently, and concisely, making an effort to avoid sounding accusatory. Encourage the other person to do the same. Maintain a respectful tone and refrain from personal attacks. Effective communication is crucial for resolving conflicts. Ensure that everyone is on the same page. Create an environment where all parties can express their concerns, interests, and viewpoints in a respectful and non-confrontational manner. Active listening, empathy, and effective communication skills are essential during this stage.

Seek compromise and collaboration: Explore solutions that cater to the needs and interests of all involved parties. Strive for win-win outcomes rather than focusing solely on winning the argument. Once the underlying issues are identified, collaborate to find a solution that satisfies everyone's needs. Be open to alternative and creative solutions.

Engage in a negotiation process where parties make concessions, offer compromises, and seek mutually agreeable solutions. The emphasis is on finding middle ground and reaching a consensus that satisfies as many interests as possible. Conflict resolution underscores the importance of compromise and collaboration, fostering a problem-solving mindset where all parties work together to find mutually acceptable solutions. Collaboration encourages understanding, empathy, and the exploration of shared interests and common ground.

Problem-solving orientation: Conflict resolution adopts a problem-solving orientation rather than a win-lose mindset. The focus is on finding creative and mutually beneficial solutions that address the underlying issues instead of perpetuating the conflict. Problem-solving encourages flexibility, compromise, and the exploration of alternative options.

Break down the issue at hand into smaller, manageable components. Collaboratively brainstorm potential solutions and evaluate their pros and cons. Encourage creativity and openness to new ideas. Engage in collaborative problem-solving to explore various options and solutions that can address the needs and interests of all parties involved. This may involve brainstorming, analyzing alternatives, and seeking creative approaches.

Mediation and facilitation: In some instances, conflicts may prove too intricate to resolve without external assistance. It is essential not to hesitate in seeking mediation or other forms of support when necessary. In cases of complexity or deeply rooted conflicts, involving mediators or facilitators can be beneficial. These individuals or organizations, without a personal stake in the issue, can guide discussions and aid in discovering mutually acceptable solutions. Mediators focus on effective communication, emotion management, and impartially guiding the resolution process. They aim to find common ground and encourage agreement while facilitating open dialogue.

Mediation proves valuable in resolving conflicts, especially when emotions are heightened, or parties struggle to find common ground. A neutral third party can facilitate communication, guide the process, and help parties explore alternative solutions. Mediation empowers individuals to take ownership of the resolution process, bringing win-win outcomes.

Conflict in the workplace: Workplace conflicts can significantly impact morale, productivity, and overall organizational success. By cultivating a culture of open communication, providing conflict resolution training, and implementing effective management strategies, organizations can establish a harmonious work environment that promotes collaboration and innovation.

Conflicts in personal relationships: Conflict resolution holds equal importance in personal relationships. Through active listening, constructive expression of emotions and a commitment to compromise, bonds can become stronger, healthier, and more fulfilling.

Lead by example: As a leader, it is imperative to model the behavior the self want to see in others. Demonstrate professionalism, respect, and a willingness to listen and collaborate. There is nothing greater than leading by one's own examples.

Stay focused on the bigger picture: In the face of challenges or conflicts, it's easy to become entangled in details. However, staying focused on the bigger picture and keeping overall goals and priorities in mind is essential.

Build on lessons learned: Post-conflict resolution, reflect on the experience as an opportunity for growth, learning, and improvement. Identify effective strategies and communication techniques, using that knowledge to handle future conflicts more adeptly.

Implementation and follow-up: Upon reaching an agreement, ensure effective implementation. Resolutions only prove effective when implemented and followed through. Establish a plan for implementation, monitor progress, and address any conflicts that may arise during the process to ensure the sustainability and success of the resolution.

Conflict resolution can occur through various methods, including mediation, negotiation, arbitration, or facilitated dialogue. The specific approach used may depend on the nature and complexity of the conflict, as well as the willingness of the involved parties to engage in the process. Conflict resolution aims to turn conflicts into opportunities for growth, understanding, and improved relationships among individuals or groups.

Effective conflict resolution skills are crucial in various settings, including personal relationships, workplaces, communities, and international diplomacy. By employing constructive and collaborative approaches to conflict resolution, individuals and organizations can enhance positive relationships, improve communication, and work towards sustainable resolutions that promote harmony and cooperation.

Conflict resolution skills are vital for politicians and others alike. To effectively manage disagreements and challenges, individuals should maintain composure and professionalism, engage in active listening, identify underlying issues, seek common ground, collaborate on solutions, communicate clearly, honor commitments, and, if needed, consider seeking external assistance. These skills empower individuals to navigate conflicts successfully and find solutions that are mutually beneficial for all parties involved.

The Importance of Traditional Conflict Resolution Methods in Political Conflicts

In the tumultuous arena of politics, conflicts are as common as politicians promising things they can't deliver. But for amidst the chaos and pandemonium, there exists a beacon of hope – traditional conflict resolution methods. While the world may be advancing at breakneck speed, sometimes, old-school is the way to go, especially when it comes to sorting out political disagreements.

Espousing Tradition in a Modern World

Picture this: A room filled with stuffy politicians in their fancy suits, arguing over policies like toddlers fighting over toys. Now imagine a wise elder, adorned in traditional attire, entering the scene and bringing with them the wisdom of generations past. Suddenly, the atmosphere shifts, and there's a glimmer of hope that resolution is within reach.

The Wisdom of the Ages

Traditional conflict resolution methods are steeped in centuries of wisdom, passed down from generation to generation like a treasured family heirloom. These methods draw upon cultural norms, community values, and the collective experience of our ancestors. They remind us that sometimes the answers we seek lie not in the shiny allure of modernity but in the time-tested traditions that have stood the test of time.

A Return to Human Connection

It is easy to forget the importance of human connection amidst the noise of social media and constant connectivity. Traditional conflict resolution method brings us back to basics, emphasizing face-to-face communication, active listening, and empathy. After all, it is much harder to hurl insults at someone when you are sitting across from them, sipping tea and sharing stories.

The Role of Tradition in Political Conflicts

Now, you might be thinking, "But how does all this talk of tradition relate to the messy world of politics?"

Building Trust and Understanding

Political conflicts often arise from a lack of trust and understanding between parties. Traditional conflict resolution methods provide a framework for building trust through dialogue, compromise, and mutual respect. By sitting down together and engaging in meaningful conversation, politicians can bridge the gap between opposing viewpoints and work towards common goals.

Preserving Cultural Identity

Politics is not just about power and policy; it is also about preserving cultural identity and heritage. Traditional conflict resolution methods honor this aspect by incorporating cultural customs, rituals, and values into the negotiation process. This not only ensures that diverse voices are heard but also fosters a sense of pride and belonging among participants.

Understanding the Essence of Traditional Conflict Resolution Method

Traditional conflict resolution method is deeply rooted in cultural heritage and historical practices, offer invaluable insights into addressing and mitigating conflicts within political dominion. But what exactly do we mean by traditional conflict resolution methods, and why are they indispensable in navigating political turmoil?

Traditional conflict resolution methods encompass a diverse array of practices, ranging from mediation and arbitration to customary rituals and community gatherings. These methods draw upon time-honored wisdom passed down through generations, emphasizing dialogue, consensus-building, and restoration of harmony. In a world where political conflicts often escalate rapidly, espousing these traditional approaches can provide a much-needed anchor of stability and resilience.

The Evolution of Conflict Resolution Techniques

Over the centuries, societies across the globe have developed intricate systems for managing conflicts within their midst. From indigenous tribes in remote regions to bustling metropolises, each community has its own set of customs and traditions aimed at resolving disputes peacefully. These methods have evolved in response to changing social dynamics and external influences, yet their core principles remain deeply ingrained in the fabric of society.

Traditional conflict resolution techniques are not static; they adapt to the needs of the time while preserving cultural authenticity. In the face of modern challenges such as political polarization and ethnic tensions, these methods offer a timeless wisdom that transcends ideological divides. By incorporating elements of traditional conflict resolution into contemporary political frameworks, societies can offer greater understanding, empathy, and cooperation among diverse factions.

Harnessing the Power of Dialogue and Reconciliation

At the heart of traditional conflict resolution lies the art of dialogue and reconciliation. Unlike adversarial approaches that prioritize victory over understanding, traditional methods seek to cultivate mutual respect and empathy among conflicting parties. Whether through tribal councils, village elders, or religious leaders, these methods create spaces for open communication and collective problem-solving.

In the context of political conflict, where entrenched ideologies often fuel animosity and distrust, the need for dialogue becomes even more pronounced. By bringing together stakeholders from across the political spectrum, traditional conflict resolution methods offer a platform for constructive engagement and compromise. Instead of viewing adversaries as enemies to be vanquished, these methods encourage seeing them as potential partners in the quest for peace and justice.

Cultural Diversity and Inclusivity

One of the most remarkable aspects of traditional conflict resolution is its celebration of cultural diversity and inclusivity. Unlike standardized legal systems that may prioritize certain norms over others, traditional methods recognize the inherent value of every community's customs and traditions. Whether it is through storytelling, song, or symbolic rituals, these methods honor the unique heritage of each group involved in the conflict.

Today, globalization and technological advancements often overshadows local traditions; the preservation of cultural identity becomes increasingly vital. By incorporating traditional conflict resolution into political processes, societies can reclaim their cultural heritage while forging paths toward a more harmonious future. In doing so, they not only resolve immediate conflicts but also lay the groundwork for sustainable peace and prosperity.

From mediation and dialogue to cultural rituals and inclusive practices, these methods offer invaluable insights into addressing and mitigating conflicts within politics. By hooking the wisdom of the past and harnessing the power of dialogue, reconciliation, and cultural diversity, societies can tackle even the most turbulent political waters with resilience and grace.

CHAPTER 14

Leadership:
As a Source of Inspiration and Motivation

A leader is someone who has a clear and convincing vision for the future, possessing certain qualities and skills that enable them to effectively lead and motivate others. They are able to articulate their visions to followers and motivate them to work towards achieving it.

In management and organizational dynamics, the term "leader" and "leadership" are often used interchangeably. However, it is crucial to strike out the difference between the two to gain a comprehensive understanding of their roles and impact. While a leader embodies certain qualities and characteristics, leadership encompasses a broader concept that extends beyond an individual. Let us make a distinction and explore the significance of both in the professional domain.

Defining a Leader

A leader is an individual with the ability to guide, inspire and influence others towards a common goal. They exhibit strong communication skills, decision-making prowess, and a clear vision. Leaders are often seen at the forefront, taking charge and providing direction to their team. They possess a deep understanding of their profession, possess expertise in their field, and are adept at motivating and empowering their subordinates.

The essence of leadership

Leadership, on the other hand, is not confined to a single person. It is a collective effort that involves a group of individuals working together to achieve a shared objective. It is a process encompassing actions, behaviors, and strategies employed by individuals to guide and inspire others. Leadership provides a positive work culture, encourages collaboration, and nurtures talent within an organization or system.

The role of a leader

A leader plays a pivotal role in setting the direction, making critical decisions, and providing guidance to their team. They are responsible for creating a positive work environment that encourages growth, development and productivity. Effective leader must possess strong interpersonal skills to effectively communicate expectations, resolve conflicts and inspire their team members to reach their full potential.

The influence of leadership

Leadership possesses a wide-reaching impact that extends beyond the influence of an individual leader. It shapes the culture, values and overall success of an organization. Effective leadership promotes a sense of purpose, aligns the efforts of individuals towards a common goal, and drives organizational growth and innovation. It empowers employees, promotes collaboration, and creates an environment conducive to continuous improvement.

Developing leadership skills

While some individuals may inherently possess leadership qualities, these qualities can be developed and refined through training, experience, and self-reflection. Continuous learning, seeking feedback, and welcoming new challenges are essential for personal and professional growth as a leader. Developing emotional intelligence, adaptability, and resilience are also crucial aspects of effective leadership.

A leader as role model

A leader serves as a role model for their team, embodying the values and behaviours they expect from others. They lead by example, demonstrating integrity, accountability and a strong work ethic. A leader's action and decisions have a profound impact on the morale and motivation of their team members, influencing their commitment and dedication towards achieving organizational goals.

Leadership as a catalyst for change

Leadership acts as a catalyst for change, driving innovation and adaptation in an ever-evolving business and political setting. Effective leaders embrace change, encourage creativity, and inspire their team members to think outside the box. They bring forth a culture that values experimentation, learning from failures and embracing new opportunities. Leadership is instrumental in tackling challenges, seizing opportunities, and steering organizations towards success.

The synergy of leader and leadership

While a leader and leadership are distinct concepts, they are interdependent and complementary. A leader's effectiveness is amplified when supported by a strong leadership framework within an organization or system. Conversely, leadership without capable leaders may lack direction and fail to inspire individuals to reach their full potential. The synergy between a leader and leadership is essential for achieving sustainable success.

The fundamental difference between a leader and a follower lies in their approach to challenges. A true leader possesses a unique set of qualities that inspire and guide their team to new heights. Let us explore the key characteristics that define exceptional leaders and their impact on the team and beyond.

Key characteristics of a **LEADER**

Vision and Purpose: A leader has a clear vision of where they want to go and what they want to achieve. They inspire others by articulating a purpose and creating a sense of direction and meaning.

Vision: A leader with vision has the ability to see beyond the current circumstances and envision a better future. They can articulate a gripping and inspiring vision that motivates and guides their team towards shared goals. A strong vision helps create a sense of direction and purpose, allowing the leader to make strategic decisions that ally with their long-term objectives.

A visionary leader

- ✓ **Thinks strategically:** They have a big-picture mindset, identifying opportunities and challenges that others may overlook.

- ✓ **Communicates effectively:** Skillful at sharing their vision with clarity and enthusiasm, ensuring that every team member understands and embraces it.

- ✓ **Inspires and mobilise:** They inspire others to work towards a common vision, fostering collaboration, motivation, and engagement.

- ✓ **Adapts and evolves:** Continuously evaluate their vision, recognizing when adjustments are necessary to meet changing circumstances and incorporate new insights.

Purpose: A leader must understand their personal purpose as well as the purpose of their team or organisation. Purpose goes beyond simply achieving objectives; it reflects a deeper meaning and a sincere desire to make a positive impact in the society.

A purpose driven leader:

- ✓ **Identifies values and passions:** They reflect on their core values and passions to identify what truly drives them and gives them a sense of fulfillment.

- ✓ **Inspires authenticity:** By living their purpose and aligning their actions with their values, they encourage others to do the same, fostering an environment of authenticity and integrity.

- ✓ **Enhances motivation and resilience:** Purpose-driven leaders have a strong intrinsic motivation, allowing them to overcome obstacles, persevere in the face of challenges, and inspire their team to do the same.

- ✓ **Cultivates a positive culture:** They create a work environment where team members feel a sense of meaning, belonging and fulfillment, leading to higher levels of engagement and productivity.

Both vision and purpose are crucial for effective leadership. A leader possessing these attributes can motivate and guide their team, navigate uncertainty, and inspire others to reach their full potential, leaving a lasting impact on the organization and society.

Integrity and ethics: Leaders demonstrate integrity by adhering to strong ethical principles and values, acting with honesty, transparency, and consistency. These qualities are not just important; they are crucial for effective leadership.

Trustworthiness: Leaders with integrity gain the trust and confidence of their team members. Consistent honesty and upholding ethical standards cultivate an environment of trust, where individuals feel safe sharing ideas, concerns, and feedback. Trust is essential for building strong relationships and effective teamwork.

Setting examples: Leaders are role model for followers, and their actions speak louder than words. When leaders lead with integrity, they set a positive example for their team members to follow. By demonstrating ethical behaviour, they inspire others to act ethically and create a culture of integrity in the organisation.

Transparency and accountability: Ethical leaders clinch transparency and hold themselves accountable for their decisions and actions. They communicate openly, share relevant information, and involve team members in decision-making when appropriate. This generates a trustful environment, where individuals feel informed and included in the organization's activities.

Moral campus: Leaders with integrity have a strong moral compass, guiding them to make ethical decisions even in challenging times. They consider the impact of their actions on various stakeholders and prioritise the greater good. Their ethical decision-making process ensures fairness, equality, and justices are upheld.

Long-term credibility: Leaders who consistently demonstrates integrity and ethical behaviour earn long-term credibility and respect from their team members, peers, and stakeholders. This credibility becomes an asset, enabling leaders to influence others, gain support and shove complex situations effectively.

Organizational culture: Leaders shape the culture of their organisation, and an ethical leader creates an ethical culture.

When integrity and ethics are central values within an organisation, it attracts individuals who share these values and promotes and environment of high ethical standards, where everyone is expected to act with integrity.

Leaders with integrity and ethics inspire trust, promote transparency and accountability, set example, rely on a strong moral compass, establish long-term credibility and shape ethical culture. By embodying these features, leaders become effective at guiding their organisations towards success while upholding ethical standards and promoting the well-being of their team members and stakeholders.

Communication and empathy: Effective leaders are skilled communicators. They listen actively, express themselves clearly, and adapt their communication style to connect with different individuals and groups. They also demonstrate empathy, understanding the emotions and perspectives of others. An empathetic leader demonstrates the ability to understand and relate to the experiences and emotions of their team members. They genuinely care about their well-being, taking into consideration their individual circumstances and perspectives.

Here are some reasons why communication and empathy are essential attributes for leaders:

Building relationships: Effective communication builds strong relationships between the leader and team members. By clearly expressing thoughts and actively listening, a leader can bring about open dialogue and create an atmosphere of trust and cooperation.

Resolving conflicts: Conflict is inevitable in any group setting, but a leader who communicates well and empathizes with different viewpoints can help resolve conflicts more effectively.

Inspiring and motivating: A leader who can effectively articulate their vision and goals can rally individuals towards a common objective. Empathy allows a leader to understand the unique situations and challenges faced by their team members, empowering them to provide the necessary support and encouragement.

Establishing a positive culture: Leaders create an environment where every individuals feels valued, heard, and appreciated. This builds morale and breeds creativity and innovation.

Adapting to change: Leaders who can effectively convey information to their team members and openly address concerns help reduce anxiety and resistance to change. Empathy allows leaders to understand and support their team members through transitional periods.

Decisiveness and accountability: Leaders make timely and informed decisions, considering various perspectives and available information. They take responsibility for their actions and are accountable for the outcomes, both positive and negative.

> ➢ Decisiveness refers to the ability to make decisions promptly and confidently, even in challenging or ambiguous situations. Decisive leader analyses information, weighs various options, and takes action to move forward. This trait demonstrates confidence, competence and the ability to handle complexity.

> ➢ Being decisive instills confidence. Decisive decisions make to build and ensure trust.

> ➢ Decisiveness saves time and avoids unnecessary delays. A leader who can swiftly assess circumstances, consider different perspectives, and execute decisions avoids wastage of resources and ensures efficient progress. This trait is especially valuable during critical moments where

quick action is required to seize opportunities or address challenges.

➢ By being proactive and resolute, leaders encourage people to think creatively, take risks and make decisions within their assigned roles. This empowers to encourage a culture of innovation, adaptability and continuous improvement.

➢ Accountability, on the other hand, revolves around taking responsibility for one's actions and the outcome of these actions. An accountable leader is transparent, owns up to their successes and mistakes, and is committed to drive positive results.

➢ Accountability also plays a vital role in learning and growth. A leader who acknowledges their mistakes and learns from them demonstrates humility and a growth mindset. This encourages a tradition of continuous improvement, where individuals are encouraged to take calculated risks, learn from failures, and seek opportunities for growth and development.

➢ Moreover, accountable leaders demonstrate integrity and ensure that goals and objectives are met. They set clear expectations, establish robust monitoring systems, and provide support and resources for success. If setbacks occur, they work collaboratively with people to identify root causes, implement necessary adjustments, and recalibrate strategies to ensure progress.

Inspiration and motivation: Leaders inspire and motivate others to reach their full potential. They lead by example, setting high standards and encouraging personal and professional growth. They empower their team members, providing support, feedback, and recognition. They play a crucial role in guiding and influencing individuals and others to achieve their full self and drive towards their goals and aspirations.

Inspiring vision: A leader with inspiration and motivation possesses a clear and achievable vision for the future. They are capable of communicating this vision effectively, painting a vivid picture of what could be achieved. By articulating a captivating vision, leaders inspire others to strive for greatness and align their efforts towards a shared goal.

Positive reinforcement: Motivational leaders understand the importance of recognizing and appreciating the efforts of others. They provide regular feedback, acknowledging achievements, praising excellence performance, and offering constructive criticism when needed.

Empowering others: Great leaders empower others by delegating responsibilities and giving them autonomy to make decisions. Empowerment instills a sense of ownership, trust, and confidence in individuals, allowing them to take on new challenges and develop their capabilities. This nurturing environment fuels motivation and inspires individuals to go above and beyond their work.

Resilience and optimism: Leaders face numerous challenges and setbacks. However, inspirational leaders demonstrate resilience and maintain an optimistic outlook. They remain steadfast in their pursuit of goals, modeling perseverance and determination. Even in challenging times, their unwavering belief in the team's capabilities motivates others to overcome obstacles and reach new heights.

Adaptability and resilience: Leaders maneuver through challenges and change with resilience. They are adaptable, open to new ideas, and able to make adjustments as needed. They remain calm and composed in the face of adversity, inspiring confidence in others.

Adaptability refers to the leader's capacity to adjust their approach and mindset in response to changing circumstances. This includes being open to new ideas, perspectives, and ways of doing things. An adaptable leader accepts change and proactively seeks out innovative solutions to problems. They are flexible and are able to quickly assess new situations, identify potential opportunities, and make necessary adjustments to strategies or plans.

Moreover, an adaptable leader encourages others to embrace change and curve a culture that values continuous learning and improvement. By promoting adaptability, they empower others to be more resilient and responsive to shifting societal needs.

Resilience, on the other hand, is the leader's ability to bounce back from setbacks, challenges, or failures. Resilient leaders display mental toughness and a positive attitude, enabling them to maintain focus and motivation during difficult times. They see setbacks as learning opportunities and use them to grow and improve.

Resilient leaders also inspire others to stay determined and motivated in the face of adversity. They provide support, guidance and encouragement, helping their people builds their own resilience and overcome obstacles. By demonstrating resilience, leaders instill confidence and create a trend of perseverance and tenacity.

It is worth noting that both adaptability and resilience go hand in hand. An adaptable leader can quickly adapt to new situations and find ways to overcome challenges, while a resilient leader can bounce back from setbacks and continue pursuing their goals in an ever-changing environment.

Collaboration and team building: Leaders establish a tradition of collaboration and teamwork. They bring people together, promote cooperation, and build strong relationships. They value diverse perspectives and encourage inclusive participation.

Firstly, collaboration allows individual to work together towards a common goal by leveraging their diverse skills, knowledge and perspectives. A great leader encourages collaboration by promoting open communication, creating a supportive and inclusive trait and cultivating a sense of trust among team members. By bringing people together, a leader can harness the collective intelligence and creativity of the team, leading to better problem-solving, innovative ideas, and optimized decision-making.

Secondly, team building is essential for creating a cohesive and motivated group of individuals. A leader recognises that the strength of a team lies not only in individual talent but also in how well team members collaborate, support one another, and work towards a shared vision. Effective team building involves identifying and leveraging the strength of team members, promoting a sense of camaraderie and mutual respect, and providing opportunities for professional growth and development. This not only improves teamwork but also boosts employee morale, productivity, and overall satisfaction.

Furthermore, a leader who prioritises collaboration and team building weave a sense of ownership and accountability within the team. When individuals feel valued and part of a team, they become more committed to achieving common goals and are willing to go extra mile to support their colleagues. This results in enhanced team performance and an increased likelihood of achieving organizational objectives.

Continuous learning and growth: Leaders are committed to continuous learning and self-improvement. They seek opportunities for personal and professional development, being updated on contextual trends and expanding their knowledge and skills. As the world rapidly evolves, leaders must adapt and stay ahead of the curve. These may include reading books, participating in workshops or conferences, seeking mentors, attending webinars, pursuing further education, encouraging feedbacks and reflection, and encouraging a culture of learning within the organisation.

Continuous learning and growth are essential characteristics of a leader. Employing a growth mindset, adapting to change, stimulating innovation, building resilience, inspiring others and improving decision-making are all benefits derived from this commitment to ongoing growth. Effective leaders understand that their personal growth positively influences their team, organisation and overall success.

Leadership is not solely determined by a title or position, but rather by the actions, influence, and impact a person has on others. Effective leadership inspires and empowers individuals and groups to achieve collective goals, bringing positive change, and make a difference in the lives of others.

LEADERSHIP

Leadership refers to the ability and process of guiding, inspiring, and influencing individuals or groups towards achieving a common goal or vision. It involves the skills, qualities, and actions that enable a person to lead and motivate others effectively.

Leadership is not limited to a specific role or position but can be demonstrated at various levels and in different contexts, including within organizations, communities, and personal relationships. A leader sets a direction, creates a sense of purpose, and guides others towards achieving shared objectives.

The nature of leadership can be complex and multifaceted, as it encompasses various qualities, behaviours and responsibilities. At its core, leadership involves guiding and inspiring a group of individuals towards achieving a common goal. It is about influencing others to move in a particular direction and bringing out the best in people to achieve desired outcomes.

Leadership can take different forms, depending on the context and the individual involved. Some leaders may possess innate qualities, such as confidence, charisma and vision that naturally inspire others to follow them. Others may develop their leadership skills through experience, training and personal growth. Effective leaders adapt their approach to the specific context and individuals they are leading. Overall, leadership is about positively influencing others, driving change, and achieving collective goals for the greater good.

Leadership is not solely about individual success but also about enabling the success of others. Effective leaders inspire and motivate individuals or groups, facilitate collaboration, and create an environment that encourages innovation, creativity, and growth.

A politician's role goes beyond just making policies and running the government. They have the power to inspire and motivate people to take action and bring about positive change in their communities. Their words and actions have the ability to spark hope, ignite passion, and drive people towards a common goal. But how can they effectively inspire and motivate others as a politician?

Leading by example: The foremost step in inspiring others is to lead by example. Politicians serve as role models, and the public expects them to uphold specific values and principles. It is crucial for politicians to live by the ideals they advocate, embodying honesty, transparency, and accountability. By demonstrating a genuine commitment to making a positive impact, politicians can inspire constituents and earn their respect.

Communicate effectively: Politicians wield the power of a platform to communicate with a large audience. This provides an opportunity to articulate a vision and plans for the future. The conviction of a politician becomes palpable through passionate and sincere delivery. Actively listening to the concerns and ideas of constituents generates a sense of being heard and valued, ultimately motivating people to engage in the political process.

Being authentic: One of the most powerful ways to inspire others is by being authentic. People are drawn to leaders who are genuine, transparent, and relatable. Sharing personal experiences, struggles, and triumphs with the audience can deepen the relationship with them. Authenticity not only inspires and motivates but also build trust and credibility with the constituents.

Setting realistic goals: While politicians may harbor grand visions for their community or country, it is essential to balance ambition with realism. Dreaming big is important, but setting achievable goals is equally vital. Individuals are more likely to be motivated when they witness tangible results. Breaking down a vision into smaller, realistic goals and effectively communicating them to constituents stimulates inspiration and motivation.

Recognise and appreciate others: No one achieves success alone. And as politician, it is imperative to recognise and appreciate the efforts of others. Acknowledge the hard work and dedication of the constituents, volunteers and colleagues. Publicly recognize their efforts and provide constructive feedback to aid their growth and improvement.

Create opportunities for participation: Motivation thrives when individuals feel a sense of ownership. Create avenues for constituents to actively participate in the political process, be it through town hall/community meetings, community events, or volunteer opportunities. Encourage the sharing of ideas and involvement in community change. Enthusiasm and motivation flourish when people believe they are making a meaningful impact.

Lead with courage: Leadership often demands tough decisions and bold actions. Be courageous and inspire others to follow suit. Many promising politicians fall short due to a lack of courage. Withstand pressures, face challenges, and tackle difficulties head-on for desired results.

Besides, there are other crucial and effective strategies. Building strong relationships with teams or constituents nurture inspiration and motivation. The best leaders adapt to change and capitalize on new opportunities. Flexibility and a willingness to change course whenever are essential. Grant individuals and teams the autonomy and resources needed for success. Empower them to take ownership, make decisions, and lead with purpose.

Communication of a clear vision inspires others to work passionately and dedicatedly toward shared goals. Collaboration enhances outcomes and strengthens relationships. Encourage teamwork among teams or fellow politicians for achieving common objectives. A positive work environment inspires individuals to deliver their best work. Cultivate a supportive and inclusive culture where everyone feels valued. Innovation leads to novel solutions and improved outcomes; patronize creativity and be open to new ideas. Celebrate individual and team successes to boost morale and motivation. Acknowledge and appreciate the hard work and dedication of teams or constituents.

Leadership as an ongoing process

Leadership has long been a focal point, often tied to the capacity to guide and inspire others toward a shared objective. However, the common perception frames leadership as an inherent trait possessed by only a select few. In reality, leadership transcends being merely a trait or skill; it is a continuous process. Unveiling the genuine power of leadership involves grasping it as an evolving journey.

So, what does leadership as a process entail? In simple terms, it embodies the ongoing and dynamic orchestration of influence and guidance toward a desired outcome for individuals or groups. This process comprises a sequence of actions and behaviors in constant flux, adapting to diverse situations and challenges. Importantly, this implies that anyone can cultivate and enhance their skills through this perpetual evolution.

A pivotal aspect of comprehending leadership as a process involves acknowledging its inclusivity. It extends beyond those in formal positions of authority or power, challenging the traditional narrative of leadership. Individuals, irrespective of titles or positions, can manifest leadership qualities and exert influence. This broadens the scope of leadership to encompass roles like parents, teachers, coaches, and even peers. At its core, leadership's true essence lies in the ability to inspire and guide others toward success.

The process can be likened to a journey. Commencing with self-awareness and an understanding of one's strengths, weaknesses, values, and beliefs, individuals craft their unique leadership styles aligned with personal values and goals. Progressing along this journey entails mastering effective communication of their vision, building meaningful relationships, and motivating others to join them on the path to accomplishing shared objectives.

Another crucial facet of leadership lies in its adaptability. A proficient leader comprehends that diverse situations demand different approaches. They accept change and are unafraid to take risks for the sake of success. This necessitates flexibility and the ability to think swiftly. Through continual assessment and adjustment of their actions, a leader can guide their team to success, even when confronted with unexpected challenges.

Furthermore, as a process, leadership involves empowering others. A genuine leader not only concentrates on personal success but also bolster the growth and development of those around them. They entrust tasks, offer support and guidance, and create opportunities for others to learn and thrive. This approach not only aids in achieving the desired outcome but also cultivates a positive and motivated work environment.

One of the paramount advantages of perceiving leadership as a process is its continuous nature. It is not a one-time event or a fixed state but an ongoing journey. This implies that leaders must consistently strive to enhance themselves and their skills to be effective. They must also remain open to learning from experiences and mistakes to evolve into better leaders.

Today, leadership has assumed heightened significance. With technological advancements and globalization, leaders must swiftly adapt and guide their teams in an increasingly competitive landscape. Those who accept the ongoing process of leadership possess the potential to become highly influential and successful leaders.

Leadership transcends being merely a process; it evolves into a lifestyle characterized by continuous learning and growth. Ongoing personal development is imperative for a leader to wield impactful influence. When learning ceases, the trajectory of growth and development is hindered. To effectively lead, one must wholeheartedly accept change, continuity, and adeptly navigate the intricacies of both.

Active leadership

Active leadership, also recognized as proactive leadership, constitutes a style marked by taking charge and assertiveness in decision-making and problem-solving. An active leader actively engages in every aspect of a project, from the planning phase to execution. They assume control of the situation, propelling initiatives forward rather than passively awaiting outcomes.

One of the key characteristics of an active leader is their hands-on approach. They lead by example and are not afraid to get their hands dirty to achieve the desired goals. This approach breeds responsibility and accountability.

Passive leadership

Conversely, passive leadership adopts a more laid-back approach to guiding a team. A passive leader tends to recede, enabling team members to make decisions and assume leadership roles. Prioritizing team harmony, they delegate tasks and grant autonomy to team members for independent completion.

Though passive leaders might be misconstrued as inactive or disengaged, this is not always accurate. While they may not exude the vocal assertiveness of active leaders, they possess clear visions and goals for their teams. They place trust in the abilities of their team members, providing space for independent work. This leadership style proves effective in situations where team members exhibit experience and competence, capable of autonomously handling assigned tasks.

The key differences

Now that we understand the basic style of active and passive leadership let us dive into the key differences between them.

Decision making

Active Leadership: The leader assumes a decisive role in decision-making.

Passive Leadership: Decisions are reached collaboratively with team members. While seeking input, the final decision rests with the leader.

Involvement

Active Leadership: Leaders are extensively involved in all project aspects.

Passive Leadership: Tasks are delegated, and emphasis is placed on the broader project vision. This variance influences the level of control and responsibility.

Communication

Active Leadership: Encourages open communication, fostering team members' expression of opinions and concerns.

Passive Leadership: Communication may be less vocal, focusing on essential tasks and updates.

Autonomy

Active Leadership: May adopt a more hands-on approach, limiting team members' autonomy.

Passive Leadership: Trusts team members' capabilities, providing them more freedom for independent task completion.

Response to challenges

Active Leadership: Takes charge in challenging situations, actively formulating solutions.

Passive Leadership: Adopts a more relaxed stance, often awaiting solutions from team members during challenges or crisis.

Assessing leadership styles: Active vs. Passive

The question of which leadership style is superior—active or passive—does not yield a definitive answer, as both possess inherent strengths and weaknesses. The efficacy of each style hinges on the specific situation and the characteristics of the team or organization at hand.

There are instances where the dynamism of an active leader proves crucial for propelling a team forward. Conversely, in different scenarios, a passive leader may excel at preserving harmony and empowering team members to assume leadership roles.

Ultimately, the triumph of a team or organization rests on a leader's capacity to adapt and skillfully blend elements of both active and passive leadership styles. A judicious leader discerns when to assume control and when to step back, allowing team members to lead. Striking a balance between hands-on involvements and delegating tasks is imperative for promoting a healthy work environment.

While active and passive leadership may seem antithetical, they each find a niche in the business realm. The proactive approach of an active leader can propel a team toward success, whereas the trust a passive leader places in team members cultivates a sense of autonomy and responsibility. The key lies in leaders comprehending their own style and adjusting it according to the demands of the situation, embodying the wisdom that "there is no one-size-fits-all approach to leadership".

CHAPTER 15

Personal Growth: Looking forward

Personal growth is an ongoing journey of self-improvement, development, and transformation that individuals embark upon to enrich their knowledge, skills, and overall well-being. This conscious effort entails expanding capabilities, broadening perspectives, and achieving both personal and professional goals.

Encompassing various dimensions of an individual's life—intellectual, emotional, social, and spiritual—personal growth is a lifelong expedition involving self-reflection, learning, and continuous development.

Personal growth is a crucial aspect of development as a politician. Continuous development and self-improvement are essential for politicians and other leaders alike to enhance their skills, expand their knowledge, and effectively serve their constituents.

Key aspects of personal growth

Self-Awareness: The genesis of personal growth lies in self-awareness, a process that involves understanding one's strengths, weaknesses, values, beliefs, and emotions. Honest introspection and reflection are imperative for gaining insights into one's interactions with the world.

Knowledge enhancement: Politicians must perpetually refine their understanding of political systems, policies, and current issues. Engaging in extensive research, reading relevant literature, and staying abreast of local, national, and global events empower them to make informed decisions and address the needs of constituents. Actively seeking mentorship and learning opportunities from successful politicians or leaders in diverse fields further enhances personal development.

Skill development: Personal growth entails the development and refinement of a spectrum of skills crucial for both personal and professional realms. This encompasses honing communication skills, problem-solving acumen, leadership capabilities, effective time management, adaptability, and more. Skill development becomes a cornerstone, enhancing competence and efficacy across various domains.

Proficiency in communication: They should strive to improve their ability to articulate their ideas clearly, listen actively, and engage in constructive dialogue. Public speaking skills, including delivering persuasive speeches and engaging with diverse audiences, helps politicians effectively convey their messages and connect with the public.

Nurturing emotional intelligence: Personal growth incorporates the cultivation of emotional intelligence—an integral aspect of understanding and managing one's emotions while empathizing with others. This facet encompasses self-regulation, self-awareness, social awareness, and relationship management. Emotional intelligence equips individuals, including politicians, to navigate relationships adeptly, address conflicts, and foster positive connections. By honing these skills, politicians can build trust, resolve conflicts, and generate a positive impact.

Upholding personal values and ethics: An essential facet of personal growth involves aligning actions and choices with one's values and ethical principles. This necessitates reflecting on personal values, engaging in ethical decision-making, and living in harmony with one's principles. Such alignment promotes integrity, authenticity, and a sense of purpose. For politicians, personal growth includes continuous reflection on values; ensuring decisions align with ethical principles. Actively seeking feedback, participating in ethical discussions, and upholding high ethical standards form integral components of this ongoing journey.

Goal setting and achievement: Personal growth entails setting meaningful goals and working towards their achievement. It involves identifying areas of improvement, setting specific, measurable, attainable, relevant, and time-bound (SMART) goals, and taking consistent action to move closer to those goals. Goal setting provides focus and direction for personal growth.

Relationship building: Developing strong relationships is imperative to political success. Politicians must actively cultivate trust, encourage collaboration, and nurture positive connections with constituents, colleagues, community leaders, and stakeholders. Developing interpersonal skills, empathy, and active listening capabilities significantly contribute to effective relationship building. Networking with fellow politicians and leaders serves as an additional avenue for personal growth, presenting opportunities for mentorship, collaboration, and learning from the experiences of others.

Leadership and decision-making: Continuous growth involves honing leadership skills and decision-making abilities. Learning about different leadership styles, understanding group dynamics, and developing strategies for consensus-building and problem-solving contribute to effective leadership. Politicians should also enhance their decision-making skills by analyzing information, considering various perspectives, and making well-informed choices.

Reflect on personal experiences: Taking dedicated moments for reflection on personal experiences as a politician, encompassing both successes and challenges, is pivotal for identifying areas of growth and improvement. Leadership is an ongoing journey, marked by a continual process where personal experiences play a significant role in shaping one's growth.

Seek feedback: Feedback from the team members, colleagues, constituents, and other politicians can provide valuable insights into one's leadership style and areas for improvement. Embracing openness to feedback, actively seeking input, and displaying a willingness to acknowledge mistakes contribute to continual personal growth.

Lifelong learning: For politicians, a steadfast commitment to lifelong learning is indispensable. Actively seeking opportunities for professional development, attending workshops and conferences, pursuing additional education when necessary and engaging in mentorship or coaching programs are avenues for continual growth. Lifelong learning not only broadens horizons but also fosters intellectual development and enhances professional capabilities.

Resilience and adaptability: Personal growth involves developing pliability and adaptability to regulate life's challenges and setbacks. It includes building the ability to bounce back from failures, embrace change, and thrive in the face of adversity. Resilience enables individuals to persevere and maintain a positive mindset. Accept challenges as opportunities for growth and learning. Rather than shying away from difficult situations, tackle them head-on with a growth mindset.

Self-Care and well-being: Personal growth emphasizes self-care and prioritizing one's well-being. It involves nurturing physical, mental, and emotional health through practices like exercise, relaxation techniques, mindfulness, maintaining healthy relationships, and finding a balance between work and personal life. Personal growth is a lifelong process that brings self-improvement, fulfillment, and a sense of purpose. It empowers individuals to reach their full potential, achieve personal goals, and lead a more meaningful and satisfying life.

Success requires a combination of skills, knowledge, personal growth and a host of other things. It requires dedication, hard work, and a strong commitment, and with the right strategies and approach. The development of the self is primarily the starting point for the fact that, it is from within the self, that things initially takes shape. We learn from what we see, hear, read, and do. The conglomeration of all these aspects and the basic understanding of the features of the underlying venture will definitely add up to our personal growth and an overall success.

Striving for success in politics: A guiding approach

Who doesn't aspire to achieve success?

As far as this book goes, we have explored the key traits and skills that are essential for success in politics. We have discussed the importance of building a strong network, developing excellent communication skills, and cultivating a reputation for integrity and honesty.

The challenges and obstacles confronting aspiring politicians, such as negative campaigning, media scrutiny, and fundraising pressures, have also been scrutinized. Nonetheless, we've demonstrated that these challenges can be surmounted with the right mindset and strategic approaches.

In essence, political success hinges on connecting with voters, cultivating relationships, and delivering tangible results. By steadfastly adhering to these principles and staying true to one's values and priorities, a prosperous political career becomes attainable.

Whether an individual is a seasoned politician or just embarking on this journey, this book offers valuable insights and practical tips for achieving success in politics. It doesn't proclaim a rigid "THIS IS THE ONLY APPROACH" paradigm; instead, it presents an option to be considered with a discerning perspective, aiming to make a positive impact on the community, the country, and the world.

About the Author

The writer is presently an Asst. Professor in the department of Sociology (HoD), Bailey Baptist College, Wokha. He has been into active politics for more than a decade and is presently serving as Personal Assistant of Shri. Mhathung Yanthan, Honb"le Advisor for Agriculture, GoN. He is an educator and a social worker who has served in various capacities such as, Vice President of Nagaland Catholic Youth Movement, General Secretary Wokha District Chess Association, President, Lotha Naga Cultural Society (erstwhile Kyong Naga Cultural Society), Wokha Unit, Joint Secretary, Nagaland Chess Association, served as the first Wokha District Peace Coordinator (Peace Channel), President, Lotha Youth Hoho, Finance Secretary, Team Metamorphosis (Wokha Based NGO) and many others. He is also a musician, composer and a performer.

9 798889 556456 1